THE
WATER GARDEN
month-by-month

THE
WATER GARDEN

month-by-month

ANDI CLEVELY

David & Charles

A DAVID & CHARLES BOOK

Book design by Diana Knapp

Colour and black and white artwork by Eva Melhuish and Michael Lye

Photographs: S & O Mathews pp2, 3, 8–9, 112–13; Jerry Harpur pp6–7, 62–3 (Designer:
Ernie Taylor), 100–1 (Designer: Bruce Kelly); Clive Nichols pp10–11, 50–1 (Designer:
Richard Coward), 88–9; Neil Campbell-Sharp pp18–19, 134–5; Garden Picture
Library/Ron Evans pp26–7 (The Well House, Cheshire); GPL/Steven Wooster pp38–9
(Designer: Anthony Paul); GPL/Ron Sutherland pp74–5; GPL/Brigitte Thomas pp126–7

First published in the UK in 1997

A catalogue record for this book is available from the British Library.

ISBN 0 7153 0575 1

Typeset by ABM Typographics Ltd, Hull
and printed in Italy by New Interlitho SpA
for David & Charles
Brunel House   Newton Abbot   Devon

CONTENTS

Introduction   6

JANUARY   10
Practical project: Planning a garden pond   16

FEBRUARY   18
Practical project: Making a start   24

MARCH   26
Practical project: Constructing a formal pond   32
Practical project: Restoring a neglected pond   36

APRIL   38
Practical project: Creating an informal pond   44
Practical project: Planting an informal pond   48

MAY   50
Practical project: A pond for wildlife   56

JUNE   62
Practical project: Making a bog garden   68
Practical project: Introducing fish to a pond   72

JULY   74
Practical project: Designing an oriental pond   80
Practical project: Installing and using electricity   86

AUGUST   88
Practical project: Making a miniature water garden   94
Practical project: Attracting wildlife to the pond   98

SEPTEMBER   100
Practical project: Adding special water garden features   106
Practical project: Caring for pond plants   110

OCTOBER   112
Practical project: Making water flow: 1   118
Practical project: Making water flow: 2   122

NOVEMBER   126
Practical project: Building an indoor pond   132

DECEMBER   134
Practical project: Making water flow: 3   140

Useful Addresses   142

Index   143

INTRODUCTION

 In one of the gardens I used to look after, we dug a new pond. It was not elaborate – just an irregular kidney shape, perhaps 6m x 3m (20ft x 10ft) overall, with a small island in the centre. Shortly after it was filled to the brim with water, I discovered two of our children, one a typically rebellious teenager and the other a cheerfully restless four-year-old, sitting side-by-side on the bank in totally rapt silence. And there they remained for nearly an hour as the first inquisitive dragonfly arrived to start making low-level passes over the surface.

There is a mysterious fascination about water that affects children and adults alike. We take it disgracefully for granted when it flows from a tap, but if confronted by a lively sparkling stream or cool limpid pool, we are immediately absorbed by the charm and fascination of water in a natural setting. Its influence on us remains a mystery thousands of years after ancient civilizations considered it the essential ingredient of a well-designed garden.

WATER FOR LIFE

Long before familiar Biblical images of springs and cool waters were set down, people were fascinated by this element which could reshape the landscape, creating or destroying features almost overnight. Animals and plants were dependent on it, nomads would stop wherever they could refresh themselves and their beasts, and the earliest settlements sprang up wherever fresh water was available. Water could be tamed, diverted to irrigate crops or drive simple engines; today hydro-electricity is not only a fundamental resource in many parts of the world but is increasingly favoured elsewhere as a renewable and non-polluting method of generating power.

As gardens evolved, water made an early appearance and its many facets were soon exploited in various artistic ways to make life generally more pleasant. In some cultures paradise was thought to be a tranquil water garden and attempts were made to recreate this image of another world, while in hot countries channels and canals were used to lead cool water into the shaded courtyards that offered a more pragmatic but nonetheless precious sanctuary from heat and drought. In classical and medieval times a source of water was almost a status symbol, used to power fountains and elaborate waterworks as a way of flaunting wealth and privilege. Today it is a more democratic element in garden design, available for all to use in countless imaginative ways.

Despite its almost universal appeal, not everyone has approved of water features in the garden: Francis Bacon, for example, wrote in 1625 that 'pools mar all and make the garden unwholesome and full of flies and frogs'. Most modern gardeners would disagree, replying that working or relaxing beside a pond is quality time, and that water provides both a vitality and an enchantment that no other feature can offer.

Clematis montana 'Elizabeth' clothes a wooden bridge in this well-established water garden. The cool greens of hostas and lady's mantle contrast well with the vibrant reds, yellows and pinks of Primula japonica

SAFETY

Water is an amiable element in its place and when treated with respect. In the garden you should take elementary precautions, especially with young families because water exerts an almost magnetic influence on them. The smallest children should always be supervised – slipping in the shallowest pond can have disastrous results. Older children should be taught a simple code of conduct when near the water, and this can be reinforced by safety measures such as ensuring that all paths and surfaces have a non-slip finish, rails and fences are installed where appropriate, and deep water is not easily accessible. If you are still worried about the possible implications of a full-size water garden, consider making a mini-pond instead (see pp94–5), as these all have a high safety rating.

SCIENCE AND RELIGION

Scientists explain our fascination with water by the fact that when in motion it can produce negative ions, cooling the air, dispelling irritability and giving us a sense of well-being. Different religions and cultures, on the other hand, have revered water as a life-giver and aid to contemplation, while Eastern philosophies have always regarded it as one of the fundamental elements of the natural world, symbolic of many positive forces – see Designing an Oriental Pond, p80, for example. And modern therapists emphasize the healing and influence of water on people absorbed in the unrelieved demands and complex pressures of daily life.

No wonder garden designers and horticultural suppliers have all identified water gardening as a growth area! Making a pond or water feature in the garden has never been easier, with the availability of flexible liners or ready-made plastic and fibreglass pools, inexpensive pumps and similar equipment, and a wide selection of aquatic plants and fish. As the projects in this book explain, many kinds of still and moving water features can be made to suit every setting, from a neat patio or tiny courtyard to the largest informal or wildflower garden.

THE ECOLOGY OF WATER

Wildflowers make satisfying companions for some kinds of pond, and part of the growing interest in water gardening is undoubtedly a result of concern about the state of the natural environment. In the past century as many as two-thirds of natural ponds have been lost to agriculture, urban expansion, pollution or simple neglect, and this has threatened the survival of many native plants and pond creatures. As a result many campaigns have been organized encouraging us to manage and protect natural ponds, and also to introduce water features to our gardens as habitats for wildlife.

Even a small formal pool will attract and host a variety of wildlife sooner or later, and part of the joy of looking after a pond is that it often combines the skills of the gardener with those of the amateur naturalist. The pond that so entranced my children had been designed as a wildlife pond and was later planted to attract water boatmen, caddis flies, whirligig beetles, tadpoles and all the other intriguing creatures that make pond-dipping with a net an absorbing part of childhood.

The pond was an equally important part of

A carnival of colours in the bog garden: Primula japonica *making a vivid display while the elegant white heads of zantedeschia add a note of restraint*

an existing garden, though, and by the addition of beautiful flowers such as irises, primulas and astilbes, together with flowering shrubs and a poolside rock garden, grew to complement its established surroundings. This is a key to the excitement of water gardening: you can choose from so many possibilities – whether it is the shape and style of the pond itself, the widely varying types of plants that appreciate moist conditions, or the host of additional features such as fountains, waterfalls and underwater lighting – and blend them all according to your own unique design to make a thing of great beauty.

WATER FOR ALL

Starting with fundamental questions such as the kind of pond you would like, how much space you can allocate and what it will cost to build, the projects in this book guide you through the design, marking out and excavation stages, to the principles of stocking, planting and maintaining the finished pond. As you will find out, translating a dream into reality is not difficult, for a pond is a natural living feature that just needs setting up in a sympathetic way. From that moment it will begin to evolve into a changing, secret habitat that can give you endless pleasure as you sit beside it enjoying its special magic.

SEASONS

The annual cycle of change in a water garden is very sensitive and driven almost entirely by natural light and temperature levels. It is impossible to predict exactly when frogs will spawn, lily pads first emerge from the surface or blanket weed start to multiply in the gradually warming water. Perhaps more than anywhere else in the garden you will need to watch for natural cues and signals when timing work, and inevitable variations from one year to the next mean that you have to be flexible when timing seasonal work. Under average conditions, however, the terms 'early', 'mid' and 'late' are used in this book to correspond approximately with the following months in British gardens:

SPRING	AUTUMN
Early: March	Early: September
Mid: April	Mid: October
Late: May	Late: November

SUMMER	WINTER
Early: June	Early: December
Mid: July	Mid: January
Late: August	Late: February

JANUARY

Midwinter, a time when you might expect a garden pond to look unappealingly bleak and lifeless. All the lush marginal plants have gone, together with the floating leaves of water lilies, duckweed and other aquatics. The surface of the pond can seem very bare too, for this water-air interface is a perilous place for plant and animal organisms easily injured by sub-zero temperatures, and it is no surprise that fish and most members of the water surface community – water fleas, pond skaters and other familiar fauna – have all vanished from sight.

Yet a pond at this time of year can still be breathtaking in the low winter sunlight, when bleached leaves of sedges, reeds and irises cast their clear reflections in the still water. And, embroidered with rime, fronds of ornamental grasses create a haunting winter wonderland, sparkling in the bright sunshine or standing out as eerie silhouettes on a frosty evening. Fantastic ice patterns like the surreal fractals of modern physics, marble the surface of a frozen pond, while gently moving or trickling water often freezes into strange translucent sculpture.

Water is a unique liquid, increasing in density as it cools until it reaches 4°C (34°F), below which it starts to become less dense again. This means that ice at freezing point floats on the slightly warmer water beneath. Ponds freeze from the surface downwards, a phenomenon that allows life to survive in the lower regions of the pond beneath a ceiling of ice.

It is here that duckweed, its winter leaves heavy with starch, can sink into protective dormancy among the rhizomes of other plants at the bottom of the pond. There too, larvae of winged insects and the winter forms of surface creatures spend the colder months, safe in the rich layer of decaying leaves and organic matter at the bottom. Despite appearances to the contrary, a pond is far from dead or uninteresting in the depths of winter.

tasks

FOR THE

month

VENTILATING A FROZEN POND

Stand a tin on the ice and fill it with hot water whenever you need to melt a hole

Hold a saucepan of boiling water on the surface until the ice melts

Float a ring made of hard rubber or wood on the water so that it freezes in the ice, and pour boiling water into the centre to form a hole

Install an electric pond-heating element fitted with a float to keep it at the surface

NOTE
After creating a hole, if possible, drain off a little of the water so that an air cavity is formed below the shelf of ice

---

CHECKLIST

- Protect ponds against prolonged freezing
- Check the water level for symptoms of cracked concrete
- Top up protection on frost-tender plants
- Clear windblown leaves and plant debris from the pond
- Choose and order new plants

FROZEN POND MAINTENANCE

The metabolism of pond fish slows right down in winter, to the point where they are semi-torpid and spend long periods without food. In this condition, low temperatures are rarely injurious and many fish can even survive being frozen in ice for a day or two. Prolonged freezing at the surface, however, prevents the escape of noxious gases, especially in shallower ponds if there is a deep sediment of organic plant debris. Ice thicker than about 5cm (2in) or covered with a layer of snow will prevent submerged plants from producing enough oxygen to compensate for this, and fish may suffer.

In larger ponds with areas deeper than 60cm (2ft), the lower water level will remain at around 4°C (39°F), no matter how cold the air temperatures, but even here pond sediment can alter the balance of dissolved gases, and so it is important during a prolonged cold spell to keep part of the surface of any pond free from ice (see margin). Do not break this forcibly with a hammer or by dropping heavy objects on to it: the impact is likely to create shock waves in the water which can seriously concuss fish.

The volume of water changes as it freezes and thaws, and ice can exert considerable pressure on the sides of ponds, especially those made of concrete. Designing at least one side with a gently sloping bank will allow for contraction and expansion. Floating a rubber ball or a large panel of wood on the surface provides a 'safety valve', absorbing much of the increased pressure and preventing damage to the pond walls. You can insulate very small ponds with a covering of boards and sacking (but only for a short time as prolonged darkness can harm plants and fish), or simply install an electric pond heater or submerged heating cable.

DAMAGED CONCRETE PONDS

If a concrete pond has been well designed and constructed, it should be able to withstand winter conditions, but it is always worth checking the water level after severe or prolonged freezing. If the level shows signs of having suddenly dropped, there is a strong possibility that a fracture or crack has appeared. Where the water level drops so far that aquatic life is endangered, fish will need to be transferred to an aquarium indoors and the most important plants (or samples of them) should be potted up and kept in containers under glass. Cracks are often difficult to repair or even find while the pond still contains water and plants, and since effective repair involves chiselling out the crack and filling it with mortar or a repair compound (treatment that may introduce lime into the water), it is best to wait until the warmer weather and then empty the pond completely before tackling the repair (see p37).

EFFECTIVE PLANT PROTECTION

Whereas aquatic plants and marginals rarely need much attention, bog garden species are treated in much the same way as other perennial garden plants. Their care includes routine mulching: a spring mulch helps to keep the roots cool and moist – an important part of satisfying their cultural needs – whereas covering

Winter plant protection

them in autumn helps to protect the dormant crowns and roots from freezing, which is a particular hazard in moist soils. Always use garden compost or leafmould made from autumn leaves that have been stacked for a year or two; alternatively bracken, straw (see p137) or spent hay may be used where appropriate. Check and top up this insulation occasionally during winter, as heavy rain will compact the layer and winds may blow some of it away. For best results, aim for a thickness of at least 5cm (2in) over plants.

KEEP PONDS CLEAN

Once any nearby trees are bare in late autumn, nets protecting the surface of the pond from falling leaves can normally be removed for storage. However, winter winds continually stir up leaves from elsewhere in the garden and these tend to settle on the water. Drag them out whenever they accumulate, before they can sink beyond reach – they are more use to you on the compost heap than decaying at the bottom of the pond. The same applies to waterside plants: the dead foliage of some species is ornamental and may help protect dormant roots from frost, but if it falls into the water and starts to decompose it can be as harmful as tree leaves.

CHOOSING NEW PLANTS

There is often time this month to settle down with plant catalogues and decide which species to order for spring planting. Make sure you have settled on the type of pond you want to develop, and which plants are the most suitable for different areas (see pp48–9). More common species, especially

oxygenators and floating aquatics are often available in spring from local or specialist shops, allowing you the opportunity to inspect the plants or to see them in flower, but for a wider choice you will need to buy by mail order. Responsible nurseries give details of the age and size of the plants, the method of packing and despatch, and may even suggest planting schemes. Remember that containerized stock is heavier to send but can be planted at your convenience, whereas bare-root plants need careful

handling and must be planted immediately or heeled in until the time or conditions are right. It may seem daunting venturing into a less familiar field such as water gardening and it is best to keep things simple, choosing a few recommended varieties at first. Gardens of all kinds evolve gradually, but especially water gardens which take time to establish; once you have a basic collection of thriving plants, you can then explore less familiar plants and test their suitability.

WATCH OUT FOR
Fish showing signs of activity in mild weather
In a very mild winter, fish may stir into life and begin visiting the surface in search of food. Normally their own stored reserves are sufficient to sustain them, but if the water temperature stays above 10°C (50°F) for any length of time they may be given a small amount of food. Offer them a little live Daphnia, if available at this time of year, or floating pellets so that you can check how fast they are eaten (they should be cleared in about five minutes if given at recommended rates).

ORNAMENTAL TREES FOR PONDS

Small or medium-sized trees provide shade and interest near a pond. Avoid fast-growing trees such as weeping willows and species with vigorous roots likely to penetrate pond liners. Here are just a few trees for use with smaller ponds.

Salix (willow), especially the weeping **S. caprea** 'Kilmarnock'; Also try **S. daphnoides** 'Aglaia' (violet willow) or **S. purpurea** 'Pendula' (weeping purple osier)

Betula pendula 'Youngii', small weeping birch

Populus tremula 'Pendula', small weeping aspen

Alnus glutinosa 'Imperialis', a slow-growing alder with finely cut leaves

plants
OF THE
month

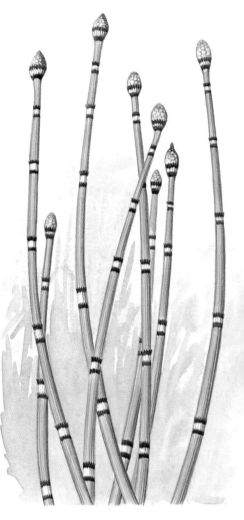

▼ WATER HYACINTH

(Eichornia crassipes,
syn. *Pontederia crassipes)*

A robust floater, irrepressible in hot climates, with beautiful orchid-like blooms appearing late in a warm summer. It is attractive for indoor cultivation as well as for ponds outdoors.

type	Tender perennial floating plant
flowers	Blue, with lavender and yellow markings, held as upright sprays well above the surface; midsummer to early autumn
foliage	Round, dark and shiny, almost succulent, with strong swollen stems honeycombed inside for buoyancy
height	30cm (12in)
spread	1sq m (3sq ft) per year
position	Full sun (cool, dull summers suppress flowering), on the surface of larger ponds; any water depth
planting	Early summer, as separate plants dropped into the water
care	Needs little attention. In a hot season thin prolific growth, and control invasiveness in warm climates where plants may become a menace. Remove in mid-autumn before the first frosts and overwinter young pieces in wet mud under glass
propagation	Division in spring, or in autumn when removed to winter quarters

(DUTCH) SCOURING RUSH, HORSE-TAIL ▶

(Equisetum hyemale, syn. *E. hibernale)*

Although many horse-tails are familiar as ineradicable weeds of wet and marshy ground, there are a few species that suit the margins of larger ponds. They are ancient plants, related to those whose decomposition has given us coal.

type	Hardy evergreen perennial; bog, marginal and shallow aquatic
flowers	Non-flowering; spores are formed in 'ears' at the tops of stems
foliage	Stiff, cylindrical stems produced from buds on creeping rhizomes, with dark nodes at intervals and no recognisable leaves
height	60–150cm (2–5ft)
spread	Up to 5m (15ft) in ideal conditions
position	Full sun or light shade; moist soil or water, depth 0–15cm (0–6in)
planting	Spring or autumn, in wet soil or shallow water. Because the rhizomes spread rapidly, confine young plants to containers or within a root barrier such as overlapping slates
care	None necessary except to restrain invasiveness by trimming around colonies occasionally with a spade
propagation	Division of rhizomes in summer
related plants	*E. arvense,* 60cm (2ft), a dwarf species with numerous whorls of intact leaves, ideal for marginal pots beside indoor ponds; *E. variegatum,* 75cm (30in), has arching stems with unusual black, green and orange sheaths to the terminal 'ears'

▼ SWEET GALINGALE
(Cyperus longus)

This is the best known of the many *Cyperus* species, members of the sedge family and all good colonizers of pond margins. They may be cut when in flower for indoor arrangements.

type	Hardy perennial; marginal and shallow aquatic
flowers	Small and reddish brown, on branching spikes; summer
foliage	Grass-like, rough and spiky, radiating in stiff terminal umbels from the tops of stems
height	90cm (3ft)
spread	30–45cm (12–18in), much more when established
position	Full sun and warmth; water depth 7.5–15cm (3–6in)
planting	Spring or autumn, in heavy soil at the pond margin for stabilizing the edge, or in a container to confine the roots
care	Can be invasive when happy, so do not grow near less robust plants that might be overwhelmed. Divide congested clumps and remove dead stems
propagation	Sow seeds in spring; divide clumps in spring or summer
related plants	*C. eragrostis*, syn. *C. vegetus* (Umbrella Grass), has broader leaves only 45cm (18in) high, with a more compact habit; ideal water depth 0–20cm (0–4in), so good for bog gardens. *C. involucratus*, syn. *C. alternifolius* (Umbrella Plant), a tall tender species, familiar as a houseplant and suitable for indoor pools; and many others, both hardy and tender kinds

WATER LETTUCE
(Pistia stratiotes)

With its origins in the tropics, this relative of the arum lily is understandably frost-shy and only happy in warm water. Its roots hang like a curtain and are a favourite haunt of spawning fish and their fry.

type	Tender perennial floating plant
flowers	Greenish, small and insignificant
foliage	Rounded with square ends, clear ribs and a velvety texture, in floating rosettes
height	5–10cm (2–4in)
spread	15–30cm (6–12in) or more
position	Water surface in all sizes of pond; minimum depth 10cm (4in)
planting	On the water surface, after the last spring frosts
care	Clusters of rosettes can spread rapidly in hot weather, but are easily controlled by division. Remove from the pond before the first autumn frosts and keep inside, in trays of moist compost or in an indoor pond or aquarium
propagation	Divide clumps of rosettes in summer

practical
project

PLANNING A GARDEN POND

MATERIALS

Concrete (p33) – very strong but difficult and onerous to lay well, especially when using shuttering, and not easy to repair; liable to frost damage depending on the design.

Rigid liner (p45) – quality and cost varies according to the material used; fairly easy to lay and repair, but the choice and size of preformed shapes is limited, and all need firm support.

Flexible liner (p57) – perhaps the most popular option; again a variety of materials reflected in cost and durability; easily laid to free-form designs although sharp corners must be avoided.

Puddled clay (p69) – a simple lining, not always available but easy to lay or repair and natural in appearance; moderately strong and easily damaged by extreme weather and tree roots.

Transforming a dream into reality needs careful planning in any area of gardening, but especially with regard to creating a pond. It is easy to devote a lot of time, money and effort to the project, only to find the result is unsatisfactory – a pond is a live habitat and for it to thrive certain preconditions must be met. Mistakes are often hard to remedy later.

FIRST PRINCIPLES

Try to define as precisely as possible what you expect from your pond. Is it to be a cool area of still water to sit by in summer, with a few fish for interest and an atmosphere of oriental tranquillity? Perhaps you would rather have one or two small features with running water to bubble or sparkle with life in a corner of the garden. Or do you want to recreate a natural pool for wildlife, stocked with all kinds of water plants and teeming with native fauna? It is important to have this kind of clear image before starting to plan.

Next, examine the site to see if your dream will harmonize easily with the existing surroundings as part of a coherent design. Some of your interesting ideas and details might have to be modified or even sacrificed altogether to maintain a unity of style. Aspects of the site which might influence your plans include:

■ Sunlight and shade – plenty of sunshine (at least 6 hours a day in summer) is vital for a healthy pond and its resident plants, although many garden species can tolerate low levels of sunlight, and a little soft shade is beneficial in high summer. Avoid the heavy shade cast by buildings and overhanging trees.

■ Very exposed areas are rarely suitable, as strong winds have a cooling influence and also increase evaporation from the water. On the other hand, do not build in a totally enclosed low-lying area that might become a frost hollow in winter.

■ Avoid obvious danger spots – nearby drains, electricity cables and water pipes, for example. Trees such as horse chestnut, laburnum, conifers and most evergreens can be poisonous; even weeping willow leaves may cause the death of pond fish, and plums or cherries are winter hosts for water lily aphids.
■ A stream or similar natural watercourse can be exploited as a water garden feature, but do not make your pond where the water table is

high unless you can organize some form of drainage: pressure of rising ground water may distort or fracture pond liners.

■ Adapt to the garden terrain. Natural contours will influence siting and shape (remember water flows downhill!), and steep slopes might need major alteration unless you can incorporate them into your design.

■ A pond is a natural focal point. You might like to blend yours into the foreground view from the house, a particular virtue if small children are likely to be playing outdoors. On the other hand, you might prefer a more secluded site for quiet contemplation.

DIMENSIONS

In your enthusiasm you may try to create the largest feasible pond – this can in fact confer advantages, because the larger its volume of water, the more stable the pond's ecosystem is likely to be. Construction costs escalate alarmingly as the pond size increases, however, and it is also important to avoid dominating the rest of the garden with an oversized area of water.

Adequate size is critical for success, depending on your plans. For example, a surface area of 1.8m² (20ft²) will be adequate for about ten fish while they are small, but they will want more as they grow (see p60); depth is equally important in this respect. Many water lilies need as much as 2m² (22ft²) for healthy development, while a fully stocked and planted pond should be at least 3.5m² (40ft²) if it is to stay clear and healthy, with a depth at some point of at least 45cm (18in), preferably 60cm (2ft). Simple formal pools, of course, can be much smaller and only a few centimetres deep.

SHAPE

This depends as much on purpose and construction as on the style of your house and garden with which the pond must harmonize. Formal ponds and those made with rigid liners can be regular and geometrical, often square or rectangular, whereas informal ponds made with flexible liners may be any shape you choose. Although a sinuous outline is attractive to wildlife, it is usually easier to keep to a simple flowing shape without sharp corners or fussy details. Vertical sides are acceptable but may cause problems in

STYLE OPTIONS

Formal ponds (pp32–3): these have clearly defined outlines in simple geometrical shapes. They are often centrepieces or integral parts of a larger formal plan, and may be used for fish and restrained plants or simply as pools of water, either still or fitted with a fountain. They may be built at ground level or as **raised ponds**, outdoors or under glass (pp132–3). **Oriental ponds** (pp80–3) are designed to look natural, but according to very formal rules.

Informal ponds (pp44–5): less stylized and planned with irregular outlines, these are intended to recreate the shape and atmosphere of natural ponds. They need space and relaxed surroundings to work effectively, and may be allowed to evolve into **wildlife ponds** (pp56–7). Possible additions include a **bog garden** (pp68–9), **rock garden** (p28) or a **waterfall** (p140).

frosty weather when ice pressure builds up, and sides sloping at about 20 degrees from the vertical are preferable. You might also want to include a shallow beach area or underwater shelves for marginal plants.

COSTS

The expense of creating a pond needs to be considered at a very early stage. Obviously larger ponds cost more to build, but it is often better to spread the work (and therefore the expense) over 2–3 years than try to make savings by omitting important features. Essential alterations and additions after the pond is built can be more expensive than including them in the initial plan, although it is a good idea to allow for expanding the pond with a bog garden, perhaps, or adding features such as lighting or a waterfall as a later option. Remember to include the cost of hiring help and equipment in your budget if the project warrants this.

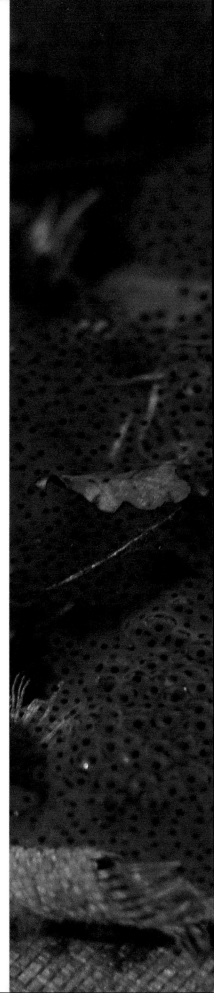

FEBRUARY

The cyclical rhythm of the garden year often pauses now. Some years the whole month is wet and bitterly cold, as if winter is reluctant to loose its grip, but other years it may turn out to be a gentle interlude that hints at the rush of new life just waiting for lengthening days and warmer temperatures.

Make the most of this brief interval before facing the challenge of early spring. In a mild spell you might begin constructing a new pond, extend an established one or start work on any necessary repairs (beware of any snap frosts if you are mixing and laying concrete). Container-grown bog plants may be planted now if the ground is not frozen or too wet, although generally it is wiser to wait until spring and to spend these weeks instead planning planting schemes and improvements for the margins of the pond.

Excavating the site of a new pond often produces huge volumes of soil that can be built up around the sides to make the foundation of a rock garden, combined perhaps with a waterfall, or beds for moisture-loving plants and bankside shrubs. Much of the charm of an informal or naturalized pond is provided by its surroundings and the complementary plants, whether these are simple cascades of aubrietia and small prostrate conifers, hugging the contours of rocks placed in the shallows, or grand lakeside associations of willows, bamboos and the huge dramatic foliage of Gunnera manicata.

Browsing through illustrated books, visualizing possible combinations and their impact on the pond or garden as a whole, and finally sketching out various design plans are all part of the exhilarating preparation that leads you from concept to creation of a whole new dimension, even in the most modest of gardens. Just a few pleasant hours spent in planning this month can set a whole agenda for the rest of the season.

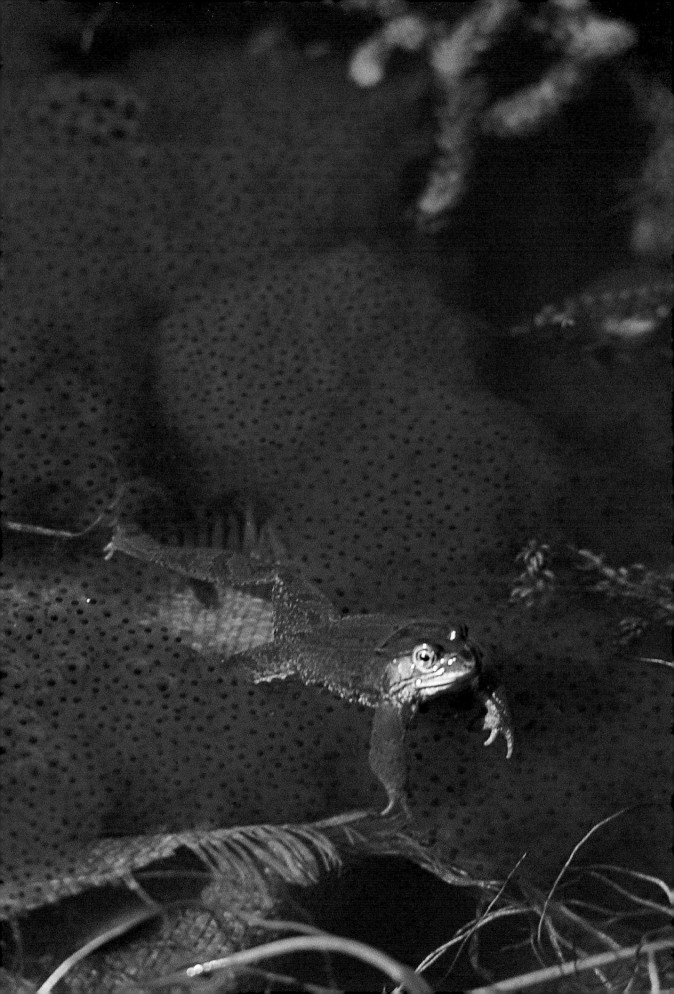

tasks

FOR THE

month

WATCH OUT FOR
Late winter flowers in the bog garden
The main burst of spring colour is still to come, which makes plants that flower now extra welcome. Dependable species include several lungworts, such as Pulmonaria angustifolia *ssp.* azurea, P. rubra *and* P. saccharata, *with their many garden forms, and also the earliest spring snowflake,* Leucojum vernum *var.* carpathicum. *If you have room for larger shrubs, plant varieties of hazel* (Corylus avellana *and* C. maxima) *and witch hazel* (Hamamelis) *for their early catkins and flowers.*

C H E C K L I S T

- Weed the bog garden
- Make a silt trap for streams and watercourses
- Watch out for early, over-amorous frogs
- Plan new ponds
- Keep overwintered plants moist indoors
- Begin a wildlife notebook
- Finish planting new trees and shrubs by the end of the month

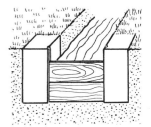

A simple sluice for the silt trap

CLEANING UP THE BOG GARDEN

The moist and organic nature of the soil in a bog garden sometimes makes weeding a very awkward operation. Hand pulling is the only effective method of keeping weeds under control and is best undertaken in summer (see p76) or after a light frosty spell when the ground is dry and more comfortable to handle. Use a small hand fork to remove obvious weeds, together with their roots, but keep an eye open for useful self-sown seedlings from choice plants: these may be left or transplanted now to other sites, or you can fork them out for potting up in a cold frame to make stronger growth before assigning them to new homes. At the same time, note which established perennials have outgrown their positions or show signs of dying back at the centre, as these will need dividing in a month or two (see pp29 & 110).

KEEPING WATER FLOWING

At certain times of the year a natural stream can turn into a raging torrent or dry up altogether. You can modify this extreme variation by installing a simple sluice at the highest point, creating a small reservoir which can also serve

as a silt trap to keep the lower water course and the running water itself much clearer.

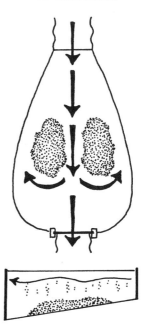

A silt trap

Shape this reservoir like an arrow head, the point facing up stream and the wide end near the sluice. This will encourage the water to swirl round and deposit any silt on the bottom, away from the sluice. Either site the reservoir in a natural depression or dig out a suitable area. For a typical small stream the area should be about 1.8m (6ft) long and 90cm (3ft) across at the widest point; the reservoir

should be about 75cm (30in) deep just behind the sluice boards, with the bottom sloping back up to the natural depth at the point of entry.

The sluice or dam can simply be a series of boards. These can be slotted one above the other between two vertical concrete posts provided with channels for the boards, or you can cement rocks together to form the walls. When the water is flowing fast, remove one or two boards to let it run away, but at other times all the boards can be kept in place to hold back a reservoir of water. Periodically the accumulation of silt will need shovelling out, and may be spread on the bog garden for its nutrient value.

EARLY COURTING FOR FROGS

In warm seasons, frogs may leave their winter quarters sooner than usual and arrive in your pond towards the end of winter. This is the start of their explosive seasonal courtship, which is usually marked by loud croaking, lively chases and splashing around in the water, often stirring up large quantities of mud and disturbing the resident flora and fauna — over-amorous males have even been sighted chasing fish instead of female frogs. Little damage is done by all this activity, which is fascinating to watch and record, and before long the adults will leave the pond again after spawning.

PLANNING NEW PONDS

This is still a relatively leisurely time of the pond year, and therefore a good opportunity to test some of your ideas for a new pond before starting construction. There are a number of factors to take into account (see pp16–17), but after considering all these it is a good idea to try the proposed layout on site to see if it is as satisfying as you expected. Use pegs and string, or a length of hosepipe for irregular shapes, and mark out the pond in its intended position. Leave this in place for several days and inspect it from all sides, trying to visualize the impact of the area of water and also the various plants on the surrounding garden. Consider its appearance in winter as well as summer, and modify the outline now while it is still possible to make changes. A number of practical matters are easily overlooked while drawing up plans on paper, and now is the time to consider them: are there any underground services such as drains, pipelines and cables in the way, for example, or large trees overhanging the site? Can you modify the shape in some way to reduce the cost of a liner? Is there access for machinery if you propose excavating a large pond, and where will all the waste soil go? These are all essential points to consider before beginning to dig.

MONITOR PLANTS OVERWINTERING INDOORS

Tender pond plants that were lifted in autumn for storing indoors in damp sand should have been inspected every 10–14 days during the winter, and watered occasionally to keep them slightly moist. They will now need checking more frequently for signs of life, and may have to be moved into a warmer lighter place if they are beginning to stir. This is particularly important if you want to divide or otherwise propagate them in time for planting out in late spring. Check any stored turions and bulbils taken last autumn from floating aquatics (see p103), and make sure their water levels are kept topped up. They too can benefit from a little extra warmth and light to stimulate early growth and make vigorous young plants for transfer outdoors in a few weeks' time.

OBSERVING POND WILDLIFE

Any area of water, even the smallest still pool, will quickly attract the interest of wildlife. Just which creatures arrive to colonize the new habitat will depend on the size of your pond, the variety of plants and features you have provided, and the proximity of other water bodies from which they will migrate.

If you keep a regular watch on the pond and its surroundings, say once a week for about half an hour, you should begin to notice new arrivals and changes in those already in residence as they move through their lifecycles. Note all this activity in a diary, partly for your own interest but also because a number of organizations depend on amateur observations for their records of specific natural populations — frogs, for example, or dragonflies.

In many parts of the world, wet environments are under threat and even the smallest pond offers sanctuary to many species. As the months pass, you will begin to appreciate the constantly changing community, simply by making and maintaining a garden pond, that you have established and helped protect. You will also understand the value of different plants or habitats.

A HIDE FOR FISH
At this time of year the surface of the pond is clear and fish are more conspicuous than usual. Help them hide from predators such as cats and herons by placing one or two lengths of 10cm (4in) diameter ceramic drainpipe on the bottom, where they can escape from view.

WILDLIFE AREAS OF THE POND

A number of different habitats exists in and around a pond, each with its own distinctive flora and fauna

Emergent plants (marginals) – the area of vegetation at the water's edge where specialist creatures live on leaves and stems, or use them for support when emerging from the water

Drawdown zone – in the wild this area occurs where water levels fluctuate between winter flood and summer depletion, offering habitats for special plants and insects. The bog garden is the nearest domestic equivalent

Water surface – some invertebrates live on or just below this, such as pond skaters, water measurers and lesser water boatmen

Shallow water – the richest part of the pond, less than 20cm (8in) deep with plenty of light and oxygen. Watch out for herbivorous insects and carnivores such as great diving beetles and dragonfly nymphs that prey on them

Deep water – alive with floating crustaceans, algae and fish, together with lush surface and submerged vegetation providing food and shelter

Substrate (pond bottom) – home to various larvae and decomposers that live and feed in the organic mud

plants
OF THE
month

Goldfish weed

Curled pondweed

OXYGENATORS

As mentioned elsewhere (see pp28 and 48), these plants may not be the most ornamental and are often submerged for much of the time, but their presence in ponds is vital for maintaining a well-balanced environment. Because of their variable behaviour and preferences, it is best to add a mixture, either distributed in the water in complete bunches as bought or, better, as several bunches planted in a shallow basket and lowered to the bottom.

CURLED PONDWEED
(Potamogeton crispus)

The translucent strap-like leaves, bronze-green or red, with wavy edges on wiry stems look like seaweed, especially in moving water. Small pinkish white flowers appear in spikes in mid- to late summer.

type	Hardy herbaceous perennial
position	Full sun or light shade; water depth 10–60cm (4–24in)
care	Needs to be thinned out occasionally. Plants die down to dormant buds in winter
propagation	Division in spring, or cuttings in spring and summer, weighted and thrown in
related plants	*P. pectinatus* (Fennel-leafed Pondweed) is daintier and grass-like

---

GOLDFISH WEED
(Lagarosiphon major, syn. *Elodea crispa)*

This vigorous evergreen, often sold for use in aquaria, can be invasive if not kept under control. The dark green, crisply curled leaves are packed tightly in whorls on long trailing stems.

type	Hardy evergreen perennial
position	Full sun or light shade; water depth 15–60cm (6–24in)
care	Thin drastically if plants outgrow their space. Remove straggly growth after winter and replace with fresh cuttings
propagation	Cuttings, weighted and tossed in, in spring or summer

---

CANADIAN PONDWEED
(Elodea canadensis)

A very successful and vigorous plant, sometimes invasive especially in larger ponds where it can be inaccessible. It has bright green leaves in very tight whorls on long branching stems.

type	Hardy or half-hardy herbaceous perennial
position	Full sun or light shade; water depth 10–60cm (4–24in)
care	Plants are dropped into the water in spring. Thin ruthlessly if it grows rapidly. Plants pass the winter as dormant buds on the bottom
propagation	Pieces pulled off, weighted and dropped in, in spring and summer
related plants	*E. crispa,* see *Lagarosiphon major* (opposite)

HAIRGRASS
(Eleocharis acicularis)

An underwater rush that stays firmly out of sight, settling at the bottom and spreading into a submerged lawn of short wiry 'turf'. Unobtrusive in formal and indoor ponds.

type	Hardy evergreen perennial
position	Full sun or light shade; water depth 10–30cm (4–12in)
care	Either drop bunches into the pond or plant in submerged baskets. May need thinning after a few years
propagation	Division in spring or summer

HORNWORT
(Ceratophyllum demersum)

An excellent oxygenator for deep or shady ponds. The branching stems are covered with dense whorls of bristly dark green foliage, and for most of the season float freely. Plants root briefly in spring and die back in autumn, spending winter on the bottom as dormant buds.

type	Hardy evergreen or semi-evergreen perennial
position	Full sun or partial shade; water depth 30cm–1.2m (1–4ft)
care	Bunches of cuttings are just dropped into the water in spring. Thin them as required during the season
propagation	Division or cuttings in spring or summer, see care

WATER VIOLET
(Hottonia palustris)

A beautiful plant that only flourishes where pond conditions are perfect. The mid-green feathery foliage floats just below the surface, and supports spikes of white or pale lavender flowers, 23cm (9in) high, in summer.

type	Hardy herbaceous perennial
position	Full sun or light shade; water depth 10–30cm (4–12in)
care	Individual plants are dropped into the water in spring. Thin excessive growth during the summer. Plants die down in autumn and pass the winter as dormant buds
propagation	Division or stem cuttings in summer

WATER STARWORT
(Callitriche hermaphroditica,
syn. *C. autumnalis)*

Highly efficient, remaining active much of the winter, with pale cress-like foliage in star-shaped rosettes. It is popular with fish and aquatic insects, and ideal for wildlife ponds.

type	Hardy evergreen perennial
position	Full sun or very light shade; water depth 10–60cm (4–24in)
care	Plant in spring in ponds already well-established. May need thinning annually
propagation	Division in spring; stem cuttings in spring and summer
related plants	*C. palustris* (syn. *C. verna*) dies back in winter. Prefers shallow water

SPIKED MILFOIL
(Myriophyllum spicatum)

Blue-green or brown thread-like leaves cluster in whorls on long trailing stems that often float above the surface and produce the occasional red-petalled flower.

type	Hardy evergreen perennial
position	Full sun or light shade; water depth 10–60cm (4–24in)
care	Undemanding. As plants sometimes succumb to frost, overwinter late summer cuttings in wet soil under glass
propagation	Cuttings in spring or summer, weighted and thrown in or kept over winter indoors
related plants	*M. verticillatum* (Whorled Milfoil) is similar and very hardy; *M. aquaticum* is less hardy

WILLOW MOSS
(Fontinalis antipyretica)

A reliable and adaptable moss species for most sites, although it looks best in running water. Its dark olive-green leaves support all kinds of aquatic life.

type	Hardy evergreen perennial
position	Full sun or shade, water depth 5–60cm (2–24in)
care	Bunched cuttings are simply thrown into the water, after which no attention is needed
propagation	Division in spring or summer
related plants	*F. gracilis* is smaller and quite rare

WATER BUTTERCUP, WATER CROWFOOT
(Ranunculus aquatilis)

A lovely species with fine grassy leaves below water and toothed clover-like foliage floating at the surface. Pure white 'buttercups' with golden centres appear on short stalks in early summer.

type	hardy herbaceous perennial
position	Full sun or semi-shade; water depth 10–60cm (4–24in)
care	Plants may need occasional thinning
propagation	Division or stem cuttings in spring, thrown into the water
related plants	*R. lingua* 'Grandiflorus' (Greater Spearwort), see p83

Water buttercup

Spiked milfoil

Water starwort

Willow moss

practical project

MAKING A START

MARKING OUT A RIGHT-ANGLE

■ Mark out one straight side of the pond as the base line, and along this side drive in two pegs, one at the corner and the other 3ft (90cm) away.

■ Stretch a 4ft (1.2m) piece of string from the corner peg and mark an arc on the ground.

■ Do the same with a 5ft (1.5m) length attached to the other peg, and where the two arcs cross drive in a peg: the line from this to the corner peg will be exactly at right angles to the base line.

■ You can use this 3–4–5 system to mark out further right-angled corners to complete the outline.

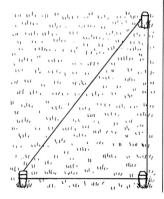

Once you have given in to the magnetic appeal of water and considered the practical implications (see p16) of constructing a pond, it is time to set your ideas down on paper, sketching in all the important details and adjusting them to fit the context of your existing garden. Drawing an accurate plan is the first of the three essential stages between concept and creation, and perhaps the most critical because a clear plan makes the following stages of marking out and excavation so much easier.

DRAFTING A WORKING PLAN

There is no need to make elaborate drawings with perspective views unless you are planning a major and complex construction, in which case it might be wiser to employ a landscape architect. The easiest way to organize your ideas is to progress in simple stages.

■ Make a rough sketch of your garden, including the position and outline of the house (remember to include the main windows and door to take account of access and views), and any hedges, paths and other prominent features.

■ Take the sketch and walk around the garden, noting important measurements such as the dimensions of the garden, the distance of the proposed pond from the house, the overall size of the pond, and the position of elements such as large trees or slopes.

■ Transfer these details to a separate sheet of paper marked out in squares (graph paper is ideal), using a simple scale: for example, 1cm/1in on the plan can represent 30cm/1ft on the ground, one square on paper can equal a square metre/yard of garden, or you might choose a scale of 1:50 (1cm=50cm).

■ Add information such as the position of drains or any heavy shade cast by trees and buildings, and then make several photocopies of this basic plan so that you can try out various different ideas (save one copy for marking up as a planting plan, see p48).

■ Finally, pencil in the outline of the pond, adjusting it to take account of all the features and equipment you want to include, such as a pump, fountain and power supply, an overflow, filter or level regulator (see pp84–5 and 101–5). Make sure it looks right in overall terms of size and scale.

MARKING OUT

Once a plan is settled, you are ready to mark out the pond's position and shape on the ground. There is still time at this stage to make final adjustments, which might be necessary if, for example, you have planned a large pond and then find when you get outdoors that the amount of room needed for access to other areas of the garden has been miscalculated. Remember that making changes now is much easier than later when excavation is under way.

■ Mark out the pond on bare ground by tracing its outline with a trail of sand trickled from the cut corner of a bag. If you are marking out on a lawn, use a length of hosepipe or thin rope and allow it to remain in position for few days after which it will leave a lasting impression where the grass has turned yellow. The necessary accuracy of the outline will depend on the method of construction – compare, for example, using a flexible liner (p56) with excavating for a pre-formed shell (p44). A formal pond with a geometric shape such as a circle or oval (see below) will need greater precision than an irregular informal one.

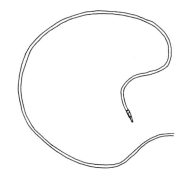

■ Walk all round the outline, view it from every angle to make sure you are satisfied with it, and leave it there for a few days to allow time for reconsideration.

EXCAVATION

■ Before starting to dig out the pond site, you will need to establish levels, because a pond that is overflowing at one end and only half full at the other will always look unsatisfactory. Even if the site seems evenly level, it is unwise to trust your eye without confirming this by measurement.

Checking levels

■ On level ground, hammer a 30cm (12in) square peg part-way into the ground at any point just outside the outline, and mark this peg in some way to identify it as the datum or reference point. Continue driving in pegs every half-metre or 18in around the pond, and check they are level with the datum point by resting a spirit level on a board across every pair of adjacent pegs. You will be able to check the depth of your excavation at any time by measuring down to the bottom from a board spanning opposite pegs.

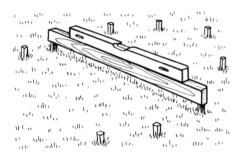

■ If the ground is sloping use longer pegs, and position the first peg at the lowest point, driving it about 10cm (4in) into the ground. Continue hammering in pegs up the slope, checking each one in the same way against the datum level and driving the higher peg further into the ground until the bubble in the spirit level is exactly central.

Digging the hole

■ For large ponds a lot of time and effort can be saved by hiring a mechanical digger, but make sure there is adequate access to the site and that you are either competent to drive the machine safely or have hired an efficient driver. It is important to have decided in advance where all the excavated soil is to go, and also to choose the right time of year for the work: a heavy machine can make a mess of your garden if the ground is soft or wet. The best times are summer while the soil is dry, or winter when it is frozen.

■ For most gardeners hand digging is the only option. Spring or autumn are the best seasons for this work, when temperatures are equable and the ground is easily dug. Allow yourself plenty of time for the job, and divide it into comfortable stages. The amount of soil to be dug out is often surprisingly large and it is a good idea to organize the work to avoid unnecessary exertion.

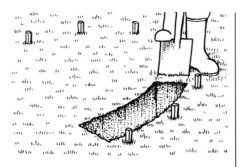

■ Skim off any turf from the surface and stack it somewhere to decompose into valuable humus. Keep the fertile topsoil separate from the less useful deeper layers; friable soil for backfilling around preformed ponds can be kept nearby on sheets of heavy plastic, while the rest may be loaded straight into a wheelbarrow for moving elsewhere.

■ Start by digging a trench all round the pond site and just inside the pegged outline; then dig out the rest of the soil to this depth right across the pond. If you have planned a marginal shelf, check you have reached this depth and then peg out a new inner outline as a guide for deeper digging. Continue until you reach the floor of the pond, measuring the final depth at several places and leaving the sides of the excavation gently sloping inwards.

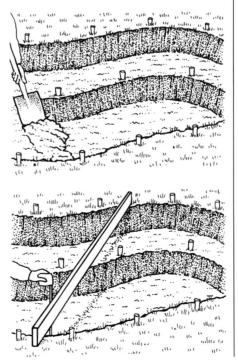

MARKING OUT A CIRCLE
This is the easiest shape to construct..
■ *Drive in a central peg, join this to a cane with a length of string the size of the pond's radius (half the diameter), and walk round the stake with the string stretched tight to mark an outline on the ground.*

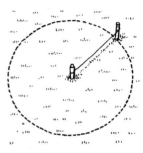

MARKING OUT AN OVAL
■ *Measure the length of the oval on the ground, push a cane into the ground at each end and join them with a length of string.*
■ *Insert a centre cane halfway along the string.*
■ *Measure two-thirds of the distance from the centre cane to each end of the string, and drive in two round pegs to mark these two intermediate points.*
■ *Stretch a piece of string from one of these pegs to the furthest end cane and back, making a loop.*
■ *Remove the three canes, and use one of these to draw the outline on the ground, with the loop as a guide around the two pegs.*

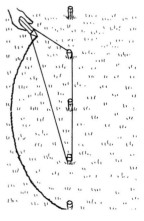

MARCH

In like a lion and out like a lamb is one traditional summary of early spring: the first days often bring winds and squally showers, whereas the end of the month can be gently benign, with the soft sunlight matching the golden colours of many spring flowers.

The pale yellow catkins of the earliest bare-stemmed willows and waterside hazels are beginning to fade, making way for the fresh acid greens of new foliage breaking out in the spring warmth. Improving conditions unlock the dormancy both of seeds and also of the buds and rhizomes that have overwintered on the bottom of the pond, stimulating new leaves of duckweed and other floating plants to begin reappearing at the surface. Water lily stems start reaching up to the light and warmth, their growth the remarkable result of a concentration of special hormones that cause the stem cells to divide rapidly and elongate until the young lily pad breaks the surface. There it begins breathing in the fresh air, abruptly dispersing those hormones that controlled its long journey from the dark cold depths.

As the resident insect life wakes up, birds may begin visiting the pond, especially insectivorous kinds such as the pied wagtail whose extraordinarily mobile tail helps it manoeuvre or brake suddenly in its restless darting pursuit of flies. All kinds of water insects appear as if by magic. Some fly in of their own accord – water boatmen and great diving beetles, for example. Others are carried to ponds on the feet of visiting birds, or may be blown there as dormant cysts or eggs from gutters, holes in the road and other impromptu pools. Minute crustaceans such as water fleas and fairy shrimps are important occupants of a spring pond, forming an essential part of its natural food chain: they are preyed on by the aquatic nymphs of damselflies, chironomids and caddisflies. These in turn feed the resident fish, also showing more signs of revival and springtime activity now.

tasks

FOR THE

month

**PLANTS FOR ROCK
GARDENS**
**Many of the marginal species
described in the Plants of the Month
pages will succeed and look well
grown among rocks by the water's
edge or in a linking pebble strip
between the rock garden and the
water. They include:**

Acorus gramineus (p130)
Ajuga reptans (p34)
Astilbe* × *arendsii (p79)
Caltha palustris (p42)
Dryopteris and other ferns
Iris sibirica (p96)
Mimulus luteus (p108)
Primula spp and hybrids (p92–3)
Trollius pumilus (p54)

**In the drier areas further from the
water, you might grow truer rock
garden species such as:**

Aubrieta* × *cultorum (aubrieta)
Aurinia saxatilis (golden alyssum)
Campanula poscharskyana
Cotoneaster dammeri
Dryas octopetala (mountain avens)
Juniperus procumbens and other
prostrate conifers
Phlox subulata
Saponaria ocymoides
Salix reticulata
Thymus serpyllum (wild thyme)

CHECKLIST

- ☐ Create a rock garden while excavating a
new pond
- ☐ Top up water levels after winter
- ☐ Plant the temperamental water violet
- ☐ Top dress established water lilies
- ☐ Divide overgrown marginal plants
- ☐ Add oxygenators to the pond (p22–3)
- ☐ Start constructing new ponds (pp24–5)

A WATERSIDE ROCK GARDEN

Disposing of the spoil
generated by excavating a
new pond site can be a
problem, and the amount of
soil removed always looks a
lot, more than the actual
volume of the hole because
soil naturally expands. If your
pond is relatively small, the
soil can usually be dispersed
around the garden.
Sometimes it is possible to
arrange with a builder to
exchange the topsoil for clay
if you are constructing a
puddled pond (see p69).

With larger earthworks, it is
best to separate the fertile
topsoil from the paler subsoil:
the latter can be carted away
for disposal, leaving you with
the good topsoil for
redistribution around the
garden. Alternatively, the
area around the pond can be
remodelled, using the subsoil
to build up new contours, and
then spreading the topsoil on
the surface for planting.

Many gardeners like to
combine making a pond with
constructing a rock garden.
This can look very attractive,
especially if it is designed to
flank a water course, perhaps
with a waterfall as the
gradient changes, or made to
slope naturally towards the
water's edge. Use the subsoil
to create the basic shape and
then set rocks in position,
wherever possible using local
stone arranged in natural
layers or 'strata lines'.

The topsoil is then mixed in
equal proportions with leafmould, peat or peat substitute,
and grit or small stone
chippings to make a planting
mixture that is spread over the
bare subsoil and rammed
between the stones. If possible
leave the rock garden over the
summer to settle and allow any
weeds to germinate and be
weeded out, before planting in
the autumn, using any of the
species that associate with
water (see margin).

TOP UP WATER LEVELS

Some gardeners like to refresh
the pond contents in early
spring when the warm weather
is approaching and life begins
to revive. The usual procedure
is to drain or siphon off
between one-third and one-half

of the water; while the level is lower, use the opportunity to remove any accumulated blanketweed and finally trim back any dead topgrowth of marginal plants that was left as protection over winter. Then gently trickle fresh water from a hosepipe into the pond to restore the normal level and dilute the concentration of salts and toxic residues that have built up during the winter.

PLANT WATER VIOLETS

It is still too early in the season to introduce the majority of plants to the pond, but one species that can be planted now is the lovely water violet, *Hottonia palustris* (see p23), a valuable oxygenator and one of the very few that produce attractive flowers. Growing it successfully can be a challenge: it needs cold, calm water and a clear, well-established pond environment with a good chemical balance (very little lime or none), so should not be added to new ponds until at least the second season. Even then it can disappear from sight for up to a year before the sudden emergence of flowers reassures you that the submerged plant is still alive. When it does bloom, the whole plant often surfaces and it is then a good idea to take cuttings from the exposed stems, rooting them in very moist compost under glass.

TOP DRESS WATER LILIES

Whereas many small pond plants seem to flourish with little care, larger species can soon exhaust available nutrients and start to decline, their foliage turning yellow and their growth becoming poor. Most marginals are best restored by division and replanting in fresh soil, but deep water aquatics, such as water lilies, can be fed at this time of year to sustain their

growth until division becomes essential (there are several ways of dividing water lilies, see p53). Sachets of proprietary fertilizer can be inserted into the soil next to the crown of the plant, or you can mix coarse bonemeal or lily fertilizer into a handful of moist clay to make a small ball for burying next to the plant. Alternatively, lift out baskets and carefully scrape

Mix coarse bonemeal or lily fertilizer with moist clay

Roll the mixture into a ball

away any surface dressing of gravel; remove some of the soil beneath, replacing this with a topdressing of fresh fertile soil or potting compost. Resurface with gravel and then return the basket to the pond.

RENEW OVERGROWN MARGINAL PLANTS

Large clump-forming marginals, such as marsh marigold, and also many creeping species will benefit from division if they have outgrown their allocated space (see p110). In very

shallow water, divisions can often be replanted immediately, either direct into the mud or in baskets, but there is often a tendency for them to float free again before they are properly rooted, and if this happens they will soon deteriorate. To avoid this, root the divisions in a greenhouse or coldframe first, replanting them later in spring as pot-grown specimens with a better chance of establishing quickly. Young segments of clump-forming marginals are rooted in 10–15cm (4–6in) pots of moist potting compost, which can be arranged in trays of shallow water on the greenhouse staging. The creeping rootstock of water mint, bog bean, and similar species can be cut into budded sections for planting in smaller pots or trays divided into separate cells, so that each young plant has a good firm rootball at planting time. Water the trays regularly or stand in a little water to keep the compost wet.

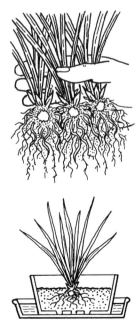

Clump-forming marginals can be divided and planted in pots of moist potting compost arranged in shallow trays of water

EASY FIRST-CLASS MARGINAL PLANTS

There is often a bewildering choice of marginal plants you can introduce to your pond, but these are some of he best.

Acorus calamus **'Variegatus'** (p130)
Alisma plantago-aquatica (p96)
Butomus umbellatus (p78)
Caltha palustris (p42)
Glyceria maxima var. *variegata* (p30)
Iris laevigata (p104)
Lysichiton americanus (p43)
Mentha aquatica (p96)
Pontederia cordata (p79)
Ranunculus lingua **'Grandiflorus'** (p85)
Schoenoplectus lacustris ssp. *tabernaemontii* (p138)
Typha minima (p139)
Veronica beccabunga (p66)
Zantedeschia aethiopica **'Crowborough'** (p116)

WATCH OUT FOR

First signs of toad-spawn
Most of us are familiar with the shapeless gelatinous masses of frog spawn, but about a fortnight after this appears you might be lucky enough to see toad-spawn in the slightly deeper water. Forming long ropes of jelly studded with round black eggs, this looks rather like strings of beads, and is often wrapped around water plants. The young tadpoles hatch after about two weeks and swim for a perilous three months in the pond before emerging as a tiny toad which may then live for up to 30 years.

Single egg-chain of the natterjack toad

Double-braided egg-chain of the common toad

plants
OF THE
month
1

▼ WATER GRASS
(Glyceria maxima, syn. *G. aquatica,*
G. spectabilis)

Keep an eye on this grassy marginal: it can be invasive and smother less robust neighbours. But it is good for stabilizing pond margins, and provides a nesting site for water birds and a spawning ground for fish. In smaller ponds grow the restrained variegated form.

type	Hardy perennial grass; marginal aquatic
flowers	Loose panicles of insignificant yellow flowers; mid-summer
foliage	Luminous green leaves, arching and flexible, up to 2.5cm (1in) wide and arising in clusters from creeping rhizomes
height	1.2–1.5m (4–5ft), flower stems up to 2.4m (8ft)
spread	60–90cm (2–3ft), but often more
position	Full sun or semi-shade; tolerates dry soil but best in a bog garden or water, depth 0–15cm (0–6in)
planting	Early spring, either direct into moist soil to stabilize banks or, for ornamental use, in containers to limit its spread
care	Easily established and undemanding; divide and replant every 4–5 years
propagation	Seed sown outdoors in spring; root division in early spring
related plants	*G.* var. *variegata* (Manna Grass), 60–90cm (2–3ft) high and spread 45cm (18in), is a popular coloured form with yellow and white stripes, and pinkish tints in spring

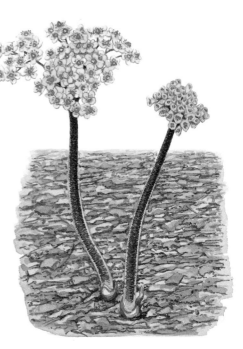

▲ UMBRELLA PLANT
(Darmera peltata, syn.
Peltiphyllum peltatum)

A highly decorative plant, with a long season of interest. The pretty flowers like those of a saxifrage appear before the new young leaves, followed by bold mounds of ornamental foliage which assumes bright copper and russet tints from late summer onwards.

type	Hardy herbaceous perennial; bog and marginal plant
flowers	White or coral-pink, on leafless stems 60cm (2ft) high; early and late spring
foliage	Bright bronzy-green and shiny, rounded, like upturned parasols, 30–38cm (12–15in) across, lobed and serrated at the edges
height	90cm–1.2m (3–4ft)
spread	90cm (3ft)
position	Full sun or semi-shade, in deep moist soil
planting	Mid-spring in deep moist soil with added humus (garden compost is ideal)
care	Deadhead after flowering and cut down faded leaves in late autumn
propagation	Divide rhizomes in spring
related plants	'Nana' (syn. *Peltiphyllum peltatum* 'Nanum'), is a dwarf form only 45cm (18in) high, ideal for smaller ponds

AMPHIBIOUS BISTORT
(Persicaria amphibia, syn. *Polygonum amphibium)*

Vigorous and adaptable wild plant that will grow happily on land as ground cover for moist soils, or in still or moving water to a great depth. An ideal subject for shading the surface of wildlife ponds.

type	Hardy evergreen perennial; marginal or deep-water aquatic
flowers	Small pink or red flowers in short, dense spikes; mid-summer to early autumn
foliage	Evergreen, lance-shaped and red tinted, floating when grown as an aquatic
height	50cm (20in)
spread	1.2m (4ft), but can sprawl more extensively
position	Full sun or shade; in bog garden, pond margins and water, depth 0–1.2m (0–4ft)
planting	Early to mid-spring
care	Cut down terrestrial clumps to ground level in mid-autumn
propagation	Root division in early spring; also self-seeds freely
related plants	Many other non-invasive species, including *P. affinis* and cultivated forms – 'Darjeeling Red', 'Donald Lowndes' and 'Superba' – these are 30cm (12in) with attractive pink or red flowers, good ground cover for bog gardens; *P. bistorta* 'Superbum', 90cm (3ft), is soft pink; *P. milletii*, 30cm (12in), is bright red

BRASS BUTTONS, GOLDEN BUTTONS
(Cotula coronopifolia)

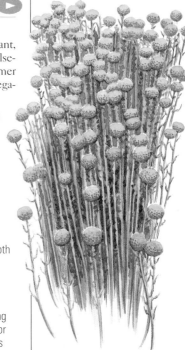

This native of Nepal is a pretty little plant, perennial in warm climates but annual elsewhere, flowering brightly from early summer until the first frosts, and usually leaving a legacy of seedlings the following spring.

type	Half-hardy annual, or short-lived tender perennial; marginal or shallow aquatic
flowers	Small, brilliant golden button-shaped blooms; all summer
foliage	Light green and aromatic, fine, bright and shining, in spreading clumps
height	15cm (6in)
spread	30cm (12in)
position	Full sun; moist soil or water, depth 0–10cm (0–4in)
planting	Seedlings transplanted in late spring
care	None necessary
propagation	Seeds sown under glass in spring and pricked out into small pots or cell trays; also self-set seedlings for transplanting

practical
project
1

CONSTRUCTING
A FORMAL POND

**PLANTS FOR FORMAL
PONDS**

The austerity of a plain pond can be
relieved with a few brightly coloured
fish, a small statue or a simple
fountain. One or two strategic
clumps of carefully chosen plants
are equally effective, but choose
varieties with care to avoid
destroying the pond's simple
symmetry. Any of the following
would be suitable, planted in
baskets in deep water or on a
marginal shelf for easy management:

Acorus calamus
Carex riparia 'Bowles' Golden'
dwarf water lilies
Eriophorum angustifolium
Houttuynia cordata
Iris kaempferi
I. sibirica
Lobelia syphilitica
Saururus tabernaemontanii
Trapa nutans
Typha minima
Zantedeschia aethiopica

The most noticeable feature of formal ponds
is that they have simple geometrical shapes,
based on symmetrical curves, straight lines
and angles. They are designed as just one
element within an overall integrated garden
plan: you might, for example, install a square
or circular pond as the decorative centre-
piece among neat flower beds, or an L-
shaped or triangular design to one side of a
patio or terrace.

SITE AND DESIGN

Wherever you choose to site it, a formal pond
will almost always be found near the house,
where it blends with the surroundings and
complements nearby shapes. A square pond
should be arranged with its sides parallel to a
nearby house wall or fence, for example, or it
can be turned at an angle to look like a dia-
mond to make a more interesting design; an
oval or circular pond within angular beds will
have a similarly dramatic impact.

Simplicity is an important design element.
Very often a formal pond can be used to give
an impression of space, because a shallow
and uncluttered area of water reflects the sky
like a mirror and appears to open up a small
garden. A long narrow pond can make a garden look wider or longer, depending on its
arrangement, but for any of these illusions to
work the water surface must be treated as
the most important feature. Keep planting to
a minimum and avoid complex shapes.

Construct and edge the pond with materials that echo those used nearby – the bricks,
concrete and timber of the house, for example, or square paving slabs like those of an
adjacent path – so that the finished effect is
one of satisfying unity. You can use a flexible
pond liner or a preformed shell, provided the
edges are hidden with a hard surfacing material (see below), or you might prefer to use concrete which is ideal for smaller formal designs
(a large pond will need shuttering to form the
sides, substantial reinforcement, efficient
tamping, and deliveries of ready-mixed concrete, and is not a do-it-yourself project).

CONSTRUCTING A CONCRETE POND

Before choosing concrete as your building
medium, remember that quite a lot of strenu-
ous work is involved: the hole must be dug
10–15cm (4–6in) deeper and wider than the finished size, and you will need to mix and barrow
many heavy loads of concrete. On the other
hand and if well-made the pond will usually
outlast those made from other materials.
Figures in brackets refer to illustration on p33.

■ Mark out and excavate the hole (see
pp24–5), shape any marginal shelves (1) and
tamp down the loosened surface with a
heavy piece of timber (2). Make sure the
sides are no steeper than about 45 degrees
to prevent the wet concrete from slipping.

■ Stabilize heavy clay that may shrink or
expand by covering it with an 8cm (3in) layer
of moist builder's sand (3).

■ Line the hole with heavy plastic sheeting,
horticultural felt, damp newspapers or a 5cm
(2in) thick base layer of lean concrete (see
margin Mixing Concrete, Mix 1), which
should be left overnight to set (about an hour
after laying, brush the surface to leave a
rough key for the next layer) (4).

■ Cover this lining with a layer of 5cm (2in)
mesh wire netting; overlap adjacent strips of
wire by about 10cm (4in), and gently tread
the layer into place (5).

■ Spread an 8–10cm (3–4in) depth of standard
concrete (Mix 2), preferably waterproofed,
over the whole area, starting at one end and
completing the work the same day (6).
Smooth the edges level (7). Leave to set for 3
weeks, protected from the sun with hessian
sacking watered regularly to keep it damp (8).

■ Finally, spread a 5cm (2in) thick finishing
coat (Mix 3) over the whole area, protect and
water as above, and leave for 10–14 days.

■ Once it has set hard, waterproof ordinary
concrete with proprietary primer and sealant,
and leave to dry. Flush out thoroughly before
filling, to remove any build-up of lime.
Complete the edging (9) (see below).

FORMAL EDGING

Stone slabs, tiles or bricks are most suitable

for edging formal ponds and are all laid in the same way. Use a bricklayer's trowel to spread a layer of waterproof mortar (Mix 3) about 2.5cm (1in) thick and the same width as the edging. Set each slab in position, a short distance from its neighbour and overhanging

the pond by about 5cm (2in). Firm or tap level with the handle of the trowel. Leave overnight and then point the joints by filling them with mortar and smoothing the surface flush. Leave to set for a week, covering the edging with plastic if rain is expected.

MIXING CONCRETE

Always mix concrete as near the site as possible, on a large board or hard surface. Aim for a stiff moist consistency. Plan the work carefully so that complete layers are finished the same day to avoid any weak joints.

Although it is possible to use the same mix throughout, greater strength will result from adjusting the ratios according to the stage of construction. Measure ingredients dry with a bucket or shovel.

- **Mix 1 Lean concrete (base layer): 7 parts 15mm (⅝in) gravel, 3 parts builder's sand, 1 part cement.**
- **Mix 2 Standard mix: 3 parts gravel, 2 parts sand, 1 part cement (+ optional waterproofing additive).**
- **Mix 3 Finishing mix: 4 parts sand, 1 part cement (+ waterproofing additive).**

CALCULATING QUANTITIES

The volume of concrete is measured in cubic metres or cubic yards.

- **Calculate the floor area of the pond, the floor area of any marginal shelf, and the area of the walls, all in square metres or yards. Add these figures together.**

- **Multiply by the thickness of concrete – e.g. for 8cm (3in) of concrete, multiply the result in square metres by 0.08 to give the volume in cubic metres, or in square yards by ⅟₁₂ to find the cubic yards.**

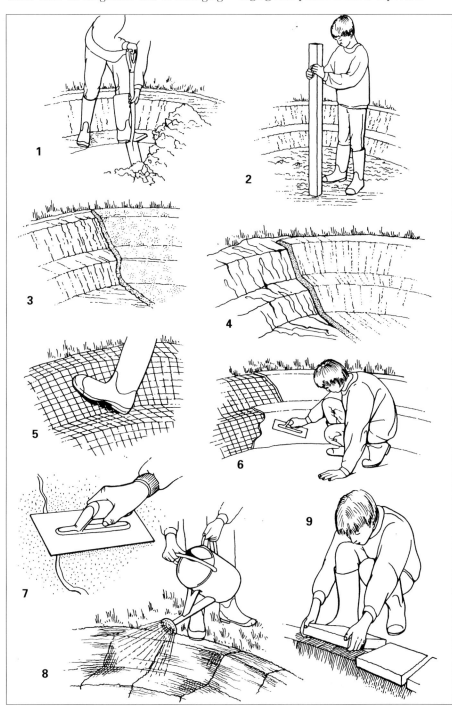

plants

OF THE

month

2

MARSH GENTIAN
(Gentiana pneumonanthe)

An unusual but very choice wild flower for damp or wet ground near the pond, and associating effectively with dainty ferns. The soil must be acid and rich in organic mattter for plants to achieve their full impact.

type	Hardy evergreen perennial; bog plant
flowers	Rich deep blue trumpet-shaped flowers in terminal clusters; late summer
foliage	Lush green, shiny and lance-shaped on short slender stems
height	30cm (12in)
spread	25cm (10in)
position	Full sun or light shade, in moist acid soil enriched with humus
planting	Spring
care	Mulch in spring with garden compost or leafmould to keep humus levels high. Acid conditions are essential, so if leaves turn yellow in summer water with sequestered iron to restore pH levels. Do not disturb clumps once established
propagation	Seeds sown under glass in early spring; soft cuttings in summer, rooted in heat

related plants	*G. asclepiadea* (Willow Gentian), 60cm (2ft), has blue flowers on taller stems and tolerates some lime in the soil; it also has a white form, 'Alba', and various pink or pale blue cultivars

(COMMON) BUGLE
(Ajuga reptans)

The familiar Bugle is an adaptable ground-cover plant that flourishes in bog gardens even more than dry sunny spots. May also be grown en masse as an alternative waterside 'lawn', or tucked in crevices between rocks.

type	Hardy evergreen perennial; ground cover bog plant
flowers	Blue or white, in conspicuous spikes; late spring to late summer
foliage	Oval and slightly crinkled, like sage, in dense mats; bright rich green in the species, variegated forms are bronze-green, reddish purple or multi-coloured
height	10–15cm (4–6in)
spread	30cm (12in) or more
position	Full sun or light shade, coloured forms full sun only; moist soil enriched with compost
planting	Autumn or spring, 15–20cm (6–8in) apart
care	No special attention needed. If invasive, outer portions may be removed at any time
propagation	Division in autumn or spring
related plants	Many fine garden forms, including 'Alba', white-flowered; 'Atropurpurea', bronze-purple leaves; 'Burgundy Glow', purple, cream, pink and green leaves; 'Multicolor' (syn. 'Rainbow', 'Tricolor'), green, red and bronze leaves; also *A. pyramidalis* 'Metallica Crispa' a slightly taller variety

HELONIOPSIS
(Heloniopsis orientalis, syn. *H. japonica)*

An attractive and curiously unfamiliar Japanese perennial, charming in spring especially when grown in bold groups near the water's edge to catch their reflection. Plants spread slowly by creeping rhizomatous root-stocks.

type	Hardy evergreen perennial; bog plant

flowers	Lilac pink and pendent, in nodding heads like bluebells on strong stems; mid- to late spring
foliage	Fresh green and spear-shaped, arranged in low spreading rosettes
height	30cm (12in)
spread	23cm (9in)
position	Light or moderate shade with shelter from cold winds, in moist soil with plenty of humus
planting	Spring, in groups 10cm (4in) apart; may take a season or two to establish
care	Cut down stems after flowers have faded or leave to set seed. Mulch in spring with compost or leafmould. Leave plants undisturbed once established
propagation	Root division in spring; seeds sown in late summer in a cold frame
related plants	*H. o.* var. *breviscarpa* has white flowers, sometimes with small plantlets at the leaf ends

SPRING SNOWFLAKE
(*Leucojum vernum*)

Easily confused with a snowdrop, snowflakes are larger plants flowering with dainty bells in spring or summer, according to the species (avoid the Autumn Snowflake, *L. autumnale*, which prefers dry conditions).

type	Hardy perennial bulb; bog plant
flowers	White with green or yellow spots, bell-shaped and nodding; late winter or early spring
foliage	Strap-like, rich green in leafy clumps
height	20cm (8in)
spread	10cm (4in)
position	Full sun or light shade; rich moist soil
planting	Early or mid-autumn, 7.5cm (3in) deep and 10cm (4in) apart in generous groups
care	Mulch in autumn and feed with general fertilizer in spring. Deadhead after flowering and divide congested clumps every 4–5 years
propagation	Seeds sown in late summer in a cold frame; division of clumps after flowering and before leaves die down
related plants	*L. aestivum* (Summer Snowflake), 60cm (2ft), is similar but larger and flowers in early summer; best form is 'Gravetye Giant'

Spring snowflake (below left) and heloniopsis (below right)

practical project 2

RESTORING A NEGLECTED POND

POLLUTED WATER
A number of factors may cause pollution in a pond. Decomposing foliage of deep-water aquatics often leaves an oily film that is easily removed by dragging newspaper or hessian sacking across the surface. Black foul-smelling water usually indicates a build-up of decaying plant material, surplus fish food or dead organisms, and this needs to be removed. To clear large accumulations you will probably need to drain the pond, but it may be possible to bail or pump out about a quarter of the water and then carefully dredge the bottom with a rake; leave the material at the edge for a day or two so that wildlife can return to the pond. Refill the pond by gently trickling in water from a hosepipe.

PROVIDING SHELTER
When restoring a pond, remember to leave some natural debris such as rotting logs and fallen leaves in strategic positions where aquatic insects can use them for food and shelter.

Reclaiming a badly overgrown and neglected pond may seem a daunting task. In serious cases the surface can be covered with a choking mass of foliage and algae, while marginal plants rampantly invade and smother each other. The water itself might be dirty or polluted, perhaps leaking from a damaged liner. The only solution would seem to be a fresh start after draining and completely cleaning out the pond.

Pause for a moment, though, before doing anything drastic. A pond might seem a wilderness in its apparent decline, but it is not necessarily dead; just as totally clearing and cultivating an overgrown garden can destroy hidden plants that might have been worth keeping, so overhauling a neglected pond could wipe out a valuable wildlife sanctuary. Ponds with a dense cover of plants are often richer wildlife habitats than open expanses of water, and the extinction of whole populations of aquatic insects and animals may result from hasty clearance.

THE CONSERVATION APPROACH

The gradual build up of silt and overcrowding plant growth that eventually turns an informal pond into a damp hollow is regarded by naturalists as a natural part of its dynamic evolution. While it might not have immediate visual appeal, a pond in this condition can still support a huge variety of plant and animal life, and may be a good example of a particular stage of development. Unless you are certain you want to overhaul and restore it totally, contact a local wildlife or conservation organization so that a survey of the pond and its surroundings can be made before any action is taken.

The result of any survey by an environmental group is likely to be a suggested management plan that takes account of your preferences as well as some of the following sensitive measures for the pond's restoration.

■ Partial removal of plant growth rather than wholesale clearance is less threatening to wildlife. Take out up to a third of any plants, but leave some areas untouched to preserve a mosaic of diverse species.

■ Leave areas of marginal plants to provide buffer zones between the pond and the rest of the garden which will provide habitats for pond animals.

■ Do not use chemicals to clear algae (blanket weed and green water) from the pond as these are detrimental to wildlife.

■ Thin overhanging tree growth, especially on the sunny side of the pond, to reduce the accumulation of dead leaves, but retain some branches to provide the light shade some creatures prefer.

■ When clearing silt from the bottom of the pond, leave one or two areas undisturbed for aquatic plants and animals.

■ Carry out the work during the autumn to minimize disruption to breeding or hibernating wildlife.

RESTORING FORMALITY

A formal pond that has fallen into disrepair can be restored to its former condition in a number of ways, which are also useful for transforming a natural pond into a more formal arrangement.

■ After checking existing populations of plants and wildlife to see if any deserve conservation, assess the condition of the structure or liner in case repair is needed; this may involve emptying the pond (see p103).

■ Decide which, if any, plants you would like to retain, and thin, divide and replant as necessary, selecting only those species that suit the proposed new design.

■ Check the edges for suitability and condition: broken or misaligned stones can be repaired, or you might prefer to replace them with new edging materials or even cover them with timber decking (see p106).

■ If you are introducing new materials or realigning the edges of the pond, try to harmonize them with nearby features. Match the angular lines of a patio, for example, or restore the nearest edge so that it is parallel to the house (see p32).

■ Replant with bold sculptural species that are non-invasive and contribute architectural features to the pond's geometrical outline. Confine more informal plants, especially those intended to attract wildlife, to the far side of the pond where they blend gently with the rest of the garden.

REPAIRING CRACKS IN CONCRETE

If a leak appears in a concrete pond, you will have to lower the water level to below the site of the crack (see p103). How you treat the problem then depends on the type of damage and its extent.

Fine cracks: fine hair-like cracks, sometimes the result of an inconsistent concrete mixture or allowing concrete to dry too fast, can often be repaired by scrubbing the surface clean and then painting it with 2-3 coats of sealant. Larger cracks should be scrubbed out and filled with waterproof mastic cement before painting with sealant.

Wide cracks: fractures wider than about 1cm (½in) need more careful repair. Clean the area and then use a cold chisel to deepen and widen the crack – cut about 2.5cm (1in) deeper than the original damage, and undercut to leave a channel that is narrower at the surface than below. Brush or blow out all the dust, and fill with waterproof mastic cement or a standard concrete mix (see p33, Mix 2) that includes a waterproofing compound. Paint with sealant after about a week.

REPAIRING A DAMAGED LINER

Exposure to sunlight can weaken **rigid liners** and cause them to crack, especially where they are installed on unstable ground. Thinner liners often become brittle and crack early in life, but even the most expensive can eventually fail as the material ages. Repair kits are available for patching damaged areas after the pond has been drained.

A flexible liner, too, has a limited life span, although when deterioration is likely to occur depends on the material used: polythene has a relatively short life and is seldom worth repairing, whereas PVC and butyl are more durable and can be patched with a repair kit. You may have to drain the pond completely (see p103) if the damage is near the bottom; otherwise empty it to just below the crack or tear so that a large enough site is exposed for patching. Clean the surface of the liner with methylated spirits before applying waterproof adhesive and a piece of repair material according to the instructions. Leave to dry before filling and restocking.

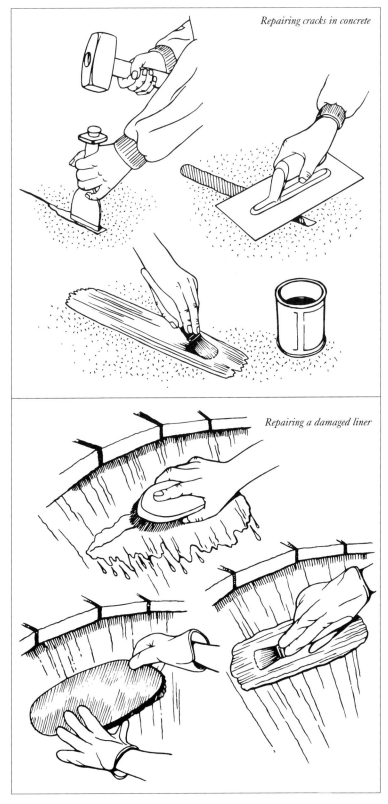

Repairing cracks in concrete

Repairing a damaged liner

APRIL

*Compared with last month's timid stirrings of life, there are real signs of
a robust and irresistible spring revival now. Temperatures and levels of
sunlight are rising steadily, rousing plants from winter dormancy.
Heralds of all this fresh vigour are the kingcups,* Caltha palustris, *whose
brilliant golden blooms appear well before most other pond plants and
feed the early bees. In the bog garden elegant stems of palest pink lady's
smock,* Cardamine pratense, *nod gracefully in the spring breeze.*

*As the water begins to warm from the surface downwards, fish become
more active, exploring regions of sunlight and shade or nosing beneath
the fresh young lily pads. It is time to start feeding them and also to
keep a watchful eye on their health, for after a sluggish winter living
on food reserves their immunity to disease is low. A green haze may
begin to fog the water, a sign that pond temperatures are high enough
to encourage the millions of minute green algae to multiply, sometimes
doubling their numbers every two or three days. Their growth
consumes oxygen and nutrients, often a benefit at this time of year since
the algal cells mop up the excess minerals that wash into the water
from the surrounding soil and help establish a more suitable chemical
balance in the water. This is all part of the normal spring cycle, and
only if the haze persists into early summer is there usually any need to
control algal growth.*

*General spring cleaning gets under way now with thinning, dividing
and replanting hardy plant species, and topping up or changing some
of the water. But spare some time for watching wildlife, which will be
as busy as you are. Summer migrant birds such as swallows and
housemartins may have discovered a handy source of building
materials for their nest, and will make frequent visits to the pond
margins to gather mud. Frog spawn and even a few tiny tadpoles
might be appearing, while dragonfly larvae start climbing stems for
their final moult after several years' feeding below water.*

tasks

FOR THE

month

☐ Spring clean ponds and equipment
☐ Test water quality and adjust if necessary
☐ Feed established plants
☐ Divide plants that are overgrown (see margin)
☐ Introduce new plants to the bog garden
☐ Sow primula seeds indoors
☐ Start feeding fish as they become active
☐ Watch out for fungal infections on fish
  (see p139)

ACID/ALKALINE TEST

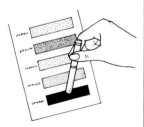

Take a beaker of pool water and pour this into a test tube; mix in some of the solution included in the kit

Check the colour of the liquid against the range of colours on the chart in the kit; this will indicate the pH value

SPRING CLEANING PONDS

Cleaning out pools thoroughly will disturb the balance of the ecosystem if done too often, and is only really necessary when neglect, overcrowding or serious disorder indicate a complete overhaul (see pp36–7). Less invasive tidying, however, is part of the spring routine as plant and animal life revives.

■ Cut down dead topgrowth remaining after the winter. Clean leaves from the netting installed in autumn, stretching and re-securing this if herons or cats are a problem. Use a rake or net to clear dead leaves and decaying plant remains from the water.

■ Raise baskets to check the quality of plants. Weak specimens will need replacement, while overcrowded or rampant plants should be divided (see p110). Overwintered bulbils and offsets (see p115) can be planted in baskets and introduced to the pond before established plants are full grown.

■ If the danger of serious frost is past in your area, remove the pool heater, clean and dry it, and then store it for the summer. Equipment such as pumps, filters and lights that were stored in the autumn should be inspected for wear

or damage before you re-install them this month in the pond.

■ Check water quality, and where ponds have become dark and cloudy or otherwise polluted, consider a partial water change to dilute accumulations of plant and fish food wastes (see p37). Top up a depleted pond to its normal level with rainwater or a gently trickling hosepipe.

TESTING WATER QUALITY

Plant and fish health can suffer if the pond water is affected by high acidity or alkalinity. This is measured on a scale of pH numbers and may be monitored easily with a pH test kit available from garden centres. A sample of the water is mixed with a reagent and the resulting colour change matched against a chart to give the pH reading – values between about 6.5 and 8.5 are acceptable.

Readings above pH8.5 indicate high alkalinity, often produced by improperly cured concrete in new pools or water draining in from limestone rocks, pebbles or reconstituted stone paving. All concrete surfaces should be sealed with pond paint (see pp32–3) and a pH buffering agent added to the water.

Very acid conditions, below

pH6.5, are usually the result of large accumulations of organic material in the pond or water draining from conifers and peaty soils nearby. Spring cleaning the pond, together with a partial water change and the addition of a buffering agent, will help restore conditions.

FEEDING PLANTS

As soon as active growth revives, established plants will need feeding; nutrients are soluble and may leach quickly from marginal beds into the water, and deep-water aquatics such as water lilies are greedy feeders that

Insert the sachet into the soil, near to the crown

Cover with gravel to prevent the fertilizer leaching into the water

benefit from a spring application of fertilizer. Take care though to avoid over-feeding plants and spillage into the water because excessively high nutrient levels encourage the growth of algae, so never scatter plant food in the water or on the surface of planting baskets.

Use a slow-release fertilizer for soil-based plants, and sachets or pellets of special aquatic plant fertilizer for submerged specimens, pushing the feed well below the gravel surface layer in baskets. Chemically based fertilizers carry the risk of raising nitrate levels in the water so where possible it is best to choose a seaweed or similarly organic feed, although these can also cause problems if applied too lavishly. Concentrate on large aquatics, marginal and bog plants, because enough nutrients usually leach into the water to feed floating plants and oxygenators.

PLANTING THE BOG GARDEN

This is a good time to introduce new bog plants – soil temperatures are rising and next month you might be too busy planting aquatics. Provided the soil has been thoroughly prepared to help retain moisture (see p68), all you need do is clear any weeds that have appeared and lightly fork the surface. If the soil is very wet, stand on a board while working to avoid local compaction.

Water the new plants in their containers, and when these have drained sufficiently remove the containers without disturbing the roots too much (tap plants out of rigid pots or use a knife to cut them free from soft plastic liners). Dig a planting hole slightly wider than the rootball, but the same depth – even a bog plant can rot if its crown is

buried below the surface. Refill the hole, firm gently and water if necessary.

SOWING PRIMULAS

There are many desirable primula species that are happy in bog garden surroundings (see p90). Seeds are often more readily available than plants and all species can be sown this month, unless you are lucky enough to obtain fresh seed which is best sown as soon as it is ripe in summer. These primulas need moist conditions at all times, so use the following method for optimum results.

- Fill shallow pots or trays with moist compost. Level the surface.
- Sow seed sparingly on the surface.
- Cover with a very thin layer of perlite so as not to exclude all light.
- Stand pots in a tray with about 1cm (½in) water in the bottom.
- Keep in a cool shaded place until seeds germinate.

- When large enough to handle, prick out individually into small pots.
- Keep seedlings moist at all times.
- Plant out in autumn or the following spring.

FEEDING FISH

The fat reserves that sustained fish during the winter will be exhausted now, and as the water warms up to 5°C (40°F) or more they will be starting to come to the surface. This is the cue to start feeding them, just a little floating food every couple of days and no more than they can clear in a few minutes – with their resistance to infection at its lowest, they need careful nurturing to restore their normal strength and energy and to bring them into good condition in time for breeding. As they become more active you can increase the quantity of food, adding high-protein supplements, such as chopped worms, live *Daphnia* and finely minced meat scraps, to the standard fish pellets or flakes.

DIVIDING PERENNIALS

Many perennials can be rejuvenated this month by simple division (see p110). Spread the work over several seasons to avoid spoiling established plantings. Indications that division is necessary vary according to plant type:

Marginals – when they become invasive (2–3 years)
Bog plants – when the centres start dying (2 years onwards)
Water lilies – fewer flowers and thin leaves (4–5 years)
Deep-water aquatics – when rootstocks outgrow baskets (3–4 years)
Floating aquatics – when congested (often annually, see p76)

SYMPTOMS OF ACIDITY (LOW PH)
- Fish prone to diseases, sudden death, red fins
- Snails develop thin pitted shells
- Oxygenating plants do not multiply well
- Biological pond filters do not work properly

SYMPTOMS OF ALKALINITY (HIGH PH)
- Fish develop fungal diseases and gill disorders
- Smell of ammonia from the water
- Plants show nutrient deficiency
- Oxygenating plants covered in slimy coating

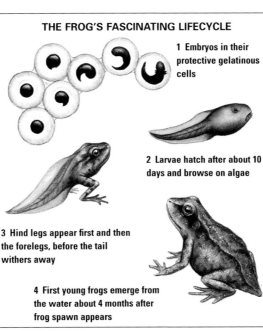

THE FROG'S FASCINATING LIFECYCLE

1 Embryos in their protective gelatinous cells

2 Larvae hatch after about 10 days and browse on algae

3 Hind legs appear first and then the forelegs, before the tail withers away

4 First young frogs emerge from the water about 4 months after frog spawn appears

plants

OF THE

month

1

▼ GOLDEN CLUB
Orontium aquaticum

This slow-growing handsome plant deserves a prominent position, centrally in a small pool or near the edge of larger ones. May be grown as a marginal plant but prefers being submerged in deeper water from which its clumps of leaves erupt dramatically.

type	Hardy perennial; marginal or aquatic
flowers	Tiny, on long white spikes with golden tips like lit candles just above water level; mid-spring to early summer; green fruits under water
foliage	Deciduous; glaucous, rounded lance-shaped, dark blue-green and silvery beneath; an erect clump in shallow water, floating or partly submerged elsewhere
height	30–75cm (12–30in)
spread	60cm (24in)
planting	Young plants in spring or dormant rhizomes in winter, in baskets as an aquatic; marginal plants need deep soil
position	Full sun or very light shade; water depth 10–45cm (4–18in)
care	Trouble-free; keep clear of more invasive plants; remove dead foliage in autumn
propagation	Sow seeds when ripe in summer, in moist soil or under glass; divide rhizomes in spring, each segment with an intact node

▲ KINGCUP, MARSH MARIGOLD
Caltha palustris

One of the most popular marginal plants, welcome for its brilliant colour and early flowering, and tolerant of a wide range of moist sites. The erect or creeping stems root wherever they touch the soil.

type	Hardy perennial; bog, marginal or shallow aquatic
flowers	Bright yellow; waxy, single and long-stemmed, about 5cm (2in) diameter; mid-spring to early summer
foliage	Deciduous; deep glossy green, round or heart-shaped and long-stalked, in neat shapely mounds
height	30–60cm (12–24in)
spread	45cm (18in)
planting	Plant early – mid-spring, about 5cm (2in) deep, in rich moist soil; use single specimens for small pools, but for a more impressive display plant them 30cm (12in) apart in massed groups beside larger pools
position	Full sun or partial shade; water depth 0–15cm (0–6in)
care	Undemanding, but beware aphids in summer and mildew in early autumn; clear foliage by late winter before new growth appears
propagation	Sow ripe seeds in moist soil, late summer or early autumn; divide spreading roots, spring or late summer
related species	*C. palustris* 'Flore Pleno', double yellow, occasionally with second flowering in autumn; *C. palustris* var. *alba*, single white, more compact and ideal for small ponds

as a bog plant; *C. palustris* var. *palustris*, very large and vigorous, 75cm (30in) – plant up to 30cm (12in) deep in large ponds

WATER FORGET-ME-NOT

Myosotis scorpioides (syn. *M. palustris*)

A common wild species of river margins, this is a cheerful and reliable plant, easily grown in most situations. Its creeping rhizomes are not invasive but will trail into the water, making this an ideal choice for masking pond edges.

type	Hardy perennial; marginal
flowers	Small and rounded, single; intense bright blue with a white, pink or yellow eye; mid-spring to late summer
foliage	Deciduous; small hairy leaves, bright green and oval, on long trailing stems
height	30cm (12in)
spread	60cm (24in)
planting	Plant in spring or summer in moist soil close to the water's edge
position	Adaptable, from full sun to heavy shade; water depth 0–15cm (0–6in)
care	Cut down dead growth in autumn; lift and divide vigorous plants every three years; watch out for aphids in summer and mildew in autumn
propagation	Divide established plants in spring; self-sown seedlings (from species only) may be transplanted in spring
related species	There are several choice forms including 'Alba', white; 'Pinkie', pink; 'Mermaid', large bright blue flowers over a long season; and 'Semperflorens', more prolific flowers and longest season of all

SKUNK CABBAGE, AMERICAN BOG ARUM

Lysichiton americanus
(syn. *Lysichitum americanum*)

A bold eye-catching plant with flowers that appear before the huge spectacular foliage. This is a bog or marginal plant to grow where its dramatic features are mirrored in the water. It is slow to flower after planting or disturbance.

type	Hardy perennial; bog garden or marginal shelf
flowers	Large, bright yellow spathes like an arum, 30cm (12in) tall
foliage	Huge and bergenia-like, with a smell of cabbages, in bold ornamental clumps
height	75–90cm (30–36in)
spread	60cm (24in)
planting	Plant in spring, 75cm (30in) apart in moist soil enriched with plenty of humus (they are very greedy plants)
position	Best in full sun but tolerates partial shade; water depth 0–10cm (0–4in)
care	Undemanding, but mulch with leaves or bracken in autumn and feed with a general fertilizer or dressing of decayed manure in spring; cut down growth in late autumn; do not disturb clumps unless essential
propagation	Sow fresh seed in moist soil, late spring or summer; self-sown seedlings (sometimes a problem) can be transplanted at any time; transplant offsets in spring
related species	*L. camschatcensis* (Oriental bog arum), a more modest plant, similar in appearance but with white 60cm (24in) spathes

practical project 1

CREATING AN INFORMAL POND

Whereas the main impact of a formal pond (see p32) depends on the pleasing symmetry of its outline, an informal pond is free and irregular in shape, perhaps to match the gentle curves of nearby flower borders or to blend with the natural and relaxed atmosphere of the rest of the garden. As with formal ponds, the water may be still or flowing, although the source of movement is more likely to be a rocky cascade or artificial stream than a fountain or canal (see p118).

The overall impression given by an informal pond is one of naturalness, not quite the apparent disorganization of the wildlife pond but more an artless and enriching interaction between water and the relaxed surroundings. Nonetheless, the initial planning is as important as for a formal pool: shape and size need to be adjusted to match the scale of the site, and to suit the contours of the ground. Remember that natural ponds tend to occur in low-lying ground, with gently varied outlines free from complicated detail.

A flexible liner (see p56) can be adapted to the free form of an informal pond, but there is also a wide selection of moulded shells, made from fibreglass or any of various rigid and reinforced plastics, that are easily and quickly installed. Sectional modules are also available for you to screw and bond together, offering scope for more creativity both in shaping the pond and in extending the project to include streams or watercourses. Remember when assessing the different models that a simple shape offers a greater surface area of water than a complex design, so increasing the scope for planting or stocking fish.

CHOOSING A RIGID LINER

A preformed pond is strong and perfectly waterproof, and is unlikely to crack or split unless subject to impact or stress, which is why the initial preparation is important. Choose a strong dark-coloured plastic or fibreglass model with a long-term guarantee, and try to buy the largest unit that will fit the allotted space, with a depth at the centre of about 60cm (24in) minimum. Most models incorporate marginal planting shelves, although these are often very narrow and you should check that their width and depth will easily accommodate planting baskets; a flat bottom is also useful for supporting baskets of deep water aquatics. Decide whether you prefer vertical or sloping sides, and if an overflow pipe or drainage plug is required.

HOW TO INSTALL A RIGID LINER

Precise digging is important with a preformed shell, especially one with a complicated shape, because all parts need equal and adequate support and there is no opportunity to make changes during excavation. Figures in brackets refer to illustration on p45.

■ Invert the shell in position and precisely scribe its outline on the ground or mark it with pegs (1). Turn it right way up and mark the corners of the bottom of the shell (2).

■ Remove the shell and then excavate the hole, making it 8–10cm (3–4in) deeper than the shell, and 15cm (6in) wider all round (this is to accommodate the sand used for packing).

■ If the pond has a shelf, reposition the shell in the hole at this level to mark the outline of the deeper portion and then continue digging to the new contour (3). Check with a straightedge and spirit level that base and shelves are both flat and level.

■ Remove any sharp stones and roots, tamp the base of the hole firmly with your feet, and level off. If there is a drainage hole, dig a trench and lay the pipe leading to a drain or soakaway (4).

■ Cover the bottom of the hole with an 8cm (3in) layer of sand; for very large ponds use a dry mixture of 85% sand and 15% cement (5). Position the liner, check for level and bed down firmly (6).

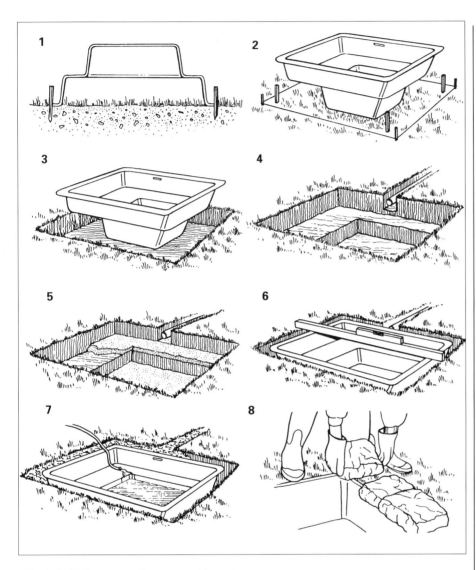

PLANTING INFORMAL PONDS

An informal pond is a more relaxed feature than a formal one, and the planting can be richer with less emphasis on restraint, simplicity and the need to clearly reveal the symmetrical outline. Bold marginal planting is appropriate, perhaps merging with a bog garden, rockery or adjacent flower bed. Almost any of the species described in this book would be suitable, including one or two water lilies according to the surface area and depth of the pond; add shallow-water marginals on the shelves and moisture-loving perennials in a bog bed next to the pond. Since the pond will most often be viewed from the house, plant the foreground more sparsely to avoid concealing the water surface, and concentrate the denser vegetation on the far side as a more natural background.

MAINTAINING RIGID LINERS

The guaranteed lifetime of the liner varies according to the quality of the material used, and may range from 3–5 years for ordinary plastics, up to 20 years or more for fibreglass. Leaking can occur after an exceptionally heavy impact, such as a large falling rock, but kits are available for repairing fractures. Little routine maintenance is needed – resist the temptation to clean the inside regularly as this will remove deposits of algae and other micro-organisms that feed aquatic wildlife.

- Partly infill the surrounding space with sand or sieved soil, and fill the pond with water to the same level to counteract any pressure on the sides (7). Moisten the infill and tamp all round to remove any air pockets.

- Finish infilling around the sides and fill the pond completely with water. If you have used sand for the infill, substitute with soil for the last 15cm (6in) if the surround is to be planted.

- Finally, mask the top of the shell with turf, slabs, rocks, plants or some other preferred edging (8). Arrange hard materials so that they project about 5cm (2in) over the water. Wait for 10–14 days before introducing water plants to the pond.

BUILDING ROCK EDGES

Informal ponds can be edged with normal garden species rather than aquatic plants because the soil around the preformed shell is no wetter than elsewhere. Paving slabs allow access to the edge of the pond but make sure they are securely bedded on mortar (see p33). To relieve the possible uniformity of paving, part of the pond can be edged with natural or synthetic rocks – do not use water-worn limestone, which is often quarried from endangered sites. Bed the rocks firmly in wet mortar to form natural groups, and set a few on the marginal shelf for greater realism: these can be rested directly on the liner, perhaps arranged round one or two baskets of marginal plants.

plants
OF THE
month
2

CUCKOO FLOWER, LADY'S SMOCK
(Cardamine pratensis)

A spring treasure that grows wild in damp meadows. It is an ideal plant for growing beside wildlife ponds or among naturalized wildflowers, and settles down well in shadier sites.

type	Hardy herbaceous perennial; bog plant
flowers	Dainty and small, pink or pale lilac, in full nodding sprays on tall stems; mid-spring to early summer
foliage	Pale green and delicately ferny, in tufted mounds
height	30–45cm (12–18in)
spread	30cm (12in)
position	Full sun or semi-shade, in moist soil or damp wildflower lawns
planting	Late autumn, 23cm (9in) apart, in natural groups
care	Mulch with compost or leafmould in early spring as growth revives. Contented plants spread steadily and also self-seed, so divide or thin out plants every few years
propagation	Seeds sown in a cold frame in spring; division of clumps in late autumn or winter
related plants	The double form 'Flore Pleno' is particularly decorative; *C. raphanifolia* (syn. *C. latifolia*), is larger, with leaves like watercress and later flowers

SNAKESHEAD FRITILLARY
(Fritillaria meleagris)

Only just a bog plant because of its native preference for damp meadows. A perfect subject for naturalizing boldly in fairly moist bog beds beside wildlife ponds. The white forms are effective massed in the shade of other plants.

type	Hardy bulb; bog and meadow plant
flowers	Chequered purple or pure white, nodding and bell-like, about 4cm (1½in) across, 1 or 2 to each narrow-leafed stem; mid- to late spring
foliage	Rich green, narrow and arching in thin clumps
height	30cm (12in)
spread	15cm (6in)
position	Light or moderate shade; tolerates dry soil but best naturalized in moist grass or among damp rocks.
planting	Early to late autumn, 10cm (4in) deep and 15cm (6in) apart (handle the flimsy bulbs carefully and do not let them dry out)
care	Feed with a general fertilizer in early spring, and leave undisturbed unless division is needed after about 4–5 years
propagation	Seeds sown as soon as they are ripe, in pots in a cold frame; small bulbils (offsets) from main bulbs in spring; division in late summer
related plants	'Aphrodite' and *alba* are white forms

LUNGWORT
(Pulmonaria angustifolia)

A familiar and attractive old cottage garden plant, often left to fend for itself in dry corners but happier in moist conditions where the speckled leaves make effective ground cover and set off the pretty spring flowers.

type	Hardy herbaceous perennial; bog plant
flowers	Bright blue fading to red, trumpet-shaped in loose heads on slightly arching stems; early to late spring
foliage	Large, matt and slightly coarse, often prominently speckled with white or cream
height	30cm (12in)
spread	45cm (18in) or more
position	Light or medium shade, in moist rich soil with plenty of humus
planting	Spring or autumn, 15–23cm (6–9in) apart, in well-prepared soil fortified with garden compost
care	Mulch in autumn with compost and again in spring with decayed leaves or grass clippings. Leave to self-seed or cut down faded flowerheads; divide and replant every 3–4 years
propagation	Division in spring or autumn
related plants	There are many cultivated forms, including 'Munstead Blue' and 'Rubra' (syn. *P. rubra*); also *P. longifolia*, which has pointed leaves, and *P. officinalis* 'Bowles' Blue', 'Cambridge Blue' and 'Sissinghurst White'

HOOP PETTICOAT
(Narcissus bulbocodium)

Fortunately a few of the wild daffodils like moist conditions, and these pretty and unusual dwarf bulbs grow naturally as drifts in streamside meadows, where their dainty inflated blooms nod cheerfully in the breeze.

type	Hardy bulb; bog and meadow plant
flowers	Broad funnel-shaped trumpets and tiny petals, bright yellow; mid-spring
foliage	Rich green, narrow and grassy in tufts
height	10–15cm (4–6in)
spread	10cm (4in)
position	Full sun; naturalized in damp grass or among wild flowers
planting	Late summer or early autumn, 8cm (3in) deep and 10cm (4in) apart, in groups
care	Undemanding: leave to set seed and spread naturally
propagation	Division mid- to late summer; bought seeds sown in pots under glass in spring, or fresh seeds when ripe in mid-summer
related plants	Various forms are available, but the commonest and best are var. *citrinus* (lemon yellow) and var. *conspicuus* (deep yellow)

practical
project
2

PLANTING AN
INFORMAL POND

There are many beautiful water plants, and once the construction of a pond is finished it is tempting to start planting lavishly and without discrimination. Take care, though: natural ponds often seem to host a huge and crowded array of species, but despite appearances these plants usually grow in organized and balanced communities, each plant with its preferred habitat and specialized function. To create a satisfying composition in and around a garden pond requires both restraint and an understanding of the importance of several different types of water plants.

WATER PLANT GROUPS

■ **Oxygenators** Perhaps the least compelling water plants, these are essential for maintaining a healthy pond environment. With the occasional exception of their flowers, all parts of the plants remain under water, where they absorb carbon dioxide and surplus minerals and so help to keep the water clear and sweet. They also produce oxygen, which most pond creatures depend on for survival.

■ **Floaters** Species such as water lettuce and water soldier drift on the surface in neat groups, whereas duckweed or fairy moss can carpet whole areas. In all cases the roots are submerged, while the leaves spread out at or just below the surface, providing welcome shade and protection for pond creatures.

■ **Marginals** These are more decorative

FILLING PONDS

A new pond should be filled with water 10–14 days before starting to plant. You will need to take care that water trickling from a hosepipe does not disturb any soil covering the bottom of the pond or a marginal shelf, and this is best done by directing the flow into a bucket or by covering the end of the pipe with a hessian sack.

plants, growing in baskets in shallow water or in the mud at the pond's edge. Their foliage and flowers form a buffer between the water and the land, offering shelter for pond life, softening the bare sides of a pond, and also providing much of the seasonal colour in a water garden. When planted direct into soil-filled marginal shelves, their roots can help to stabilize the banks.

■ **Deep water aquatics** Whereas marginals prefer the shallows near the edge, the aquatics are happiest in depths more than about 23cm (9in). Water lilies are the best known kinds, but there are other lovely species whose leaves help to shade the surface, keeping the water clear and offering shelter for pond creatures. Most ponds can only accommodate 2–3 specimens.

■ **Bog plants** Although some marginals will grow in damp ground away from the water,

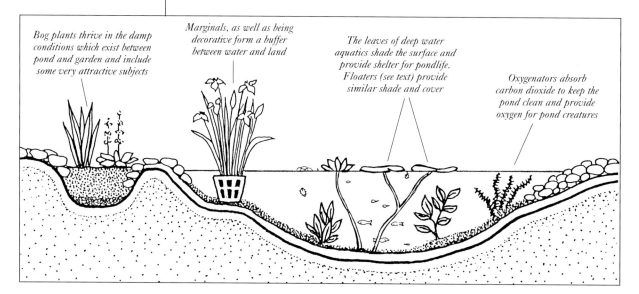

Bog plants thrive in the damp conditions which exist between pond and garden and include some very attractive subjects

Marginals, as well as being decorative form a buffer between water and land

The leaves of deep water aquatics shade the surface and provide shelter for pondlife. Floaters (see text) provide similar shade and cover

Oxygenators absorb carbon dioxide to keep the pond clean and provide oxygen for pond creatures

See also:
Autumn stems and leaves (p115)
Bedding for ponds (p137)
Buying new plants (p52)
Caring for pond plants (p110)
Choosing new plants (p13)
Easy marginal plants (p29)
Indoor pond plants (p133)
Miniature pond plants (p95)
Oriental pond plants (p80)
Ornamental trees for ponds (p13)
Planning for colour (p136)
Planting aquatics (p52)
Planting in baskets (p52)
Plants for rock garden (p29)
Tree and shrub planting (p137)
Water plants in autumn (p111)
Wildlife pond plants (p59)

SAMPLE PLANT SELECTIONS

Choosing a balanced plant population depends primarily on the available space, as these examples show.

Small pond – 0.75m² (8ft²)
5 oxygenators
2 floaters
4 marginals

Medium pond – 1.8m² (20ft²)
5 oxygenators
3 floaters
6 marginals
2 deep water aquatics

Large pond – 4.5m² (50ft²)
20 oxygenators
5 floaters
8 marginals
3 deep water aquatics

bog garden plants are moisture-loving species that cannot stand permanently waterlogged conditions, and they are usually grown in special moist beds close to the pond (see p68). This is a mixed group that includes many familiar ornamentals such as astilbes and day lilies, and forms a useful transition between the pond and the rest of the garden.

MAKING A PLANTING PLAN

In all but the smallest ponds there will be room for examples from all the groups mentioned above. Drawing up a list of the species you would like to include requires a planting plan that identifies their exact position and space needed. For convenience, it is a good idea to divide them into two groups: true water plants and those to be grown at the waterside; and it may help further to subdivide plants into large, medium-sized and small species.

First make a scale drawing of the pond and its immediate surroundings (see p24) – include trees and their dimensions, shrubs, paths and other existing features. Decide at an early stage the style you prefer (formal, natural, exotic and so on), as this will influence your selection of plants. Make a list of those plants you would particularly like, checking characteristics such as size, shape, colour and site preference.

Mark on the plan possible sites for the chosen plants, remembering to avoid potential problems such as shade from established trees or competition from invasive species. Match or contrast plants according to their height, spread and appearance, so that together they form a satisfying unity, and try to include enough evergreens to make up about one-third of the total, for interest all year round. Finally, try to visualize the overall balance and impact of the plants when mature: full-grown aquatics can cover up to two-thirds of the pond surface, marginals about one-third of the total perimeter.

COMPOSTS AND CONTAINERS

Aquatic plants do not need rich soil or compost for healthy growth, and ordinary clean garden soil is perfectly suitable unless it is very light and sandy (this tends to wash away under water). Gather it from an area that is not very fertile – a neglected corner is ideal – and sieve out any weeds, leaves, twigs and other organic material before use. Alternatively, a specially prepared, branded compost for aquatic plants can be used for filling planting containers.

Whether to grow plants in containers or to plant direct into soil is a matter for personal choice. Baskets and other containers allow you to maintain more control over plants and to remove them for examination or propagation, but in larger wildlife ponds a 15–20cm (6–8in) layer of soil spread over the bottom of the pond or just on marginal shelves supports more natural vigour. The soil can be covered with a thin layer of gravel to prevent its being stirred up by fish or water movements.

MAY

By late spring there is no longer any doubt that the season is irresistibly under way, and everywhere you look you will find proof that life has well and truly returned to the pond world.

It is now, for example, that you are most likely to see newts in the water. For much of the year they are secretive and seldom seen, only venturing out at night from their refuges under stones or in damp corners of the garden. But this month they gather in ponds to lead an altogether different aquatic life, the male becoming quite handsome with his coloured courtship crest and the female busy attaching hundreds of tiny eggs individually to the leaves of marginal plants. After only a month the adults will leave the water, for the first few weeks sheltering in moist spots near the pond before returning to their winter quarters, while their young remain in the pond as tadpoles well into autumn.

The onset of warmer weather and an increase in the natural foods in the pond also stimulate fish to spawn, an annual frenzy of activity that you might misinterpret as an outbreak of antisocial behaviour in your collection of fish. For several days males will be seen chivvying females, chasing them around and driving them into denser patches of oxygenating plants in the warmer shallows. This stimulates the release of the tiny eggs which may be found afterwards trapped among the leaves.

All this activity is the cue for you to restock the pond, now that conditions are more favourable. Provided the water and plants have had a few weeks in which to establish and stabilize, you can start introducing fish to a new pond. This is also the time to return to the open water tender plants such as tropical water lilies, water hyacinth and papyrus that have been overwintered under cover. Arums and other tender bulbs may also be set out in the bog garden to complete planting associations for the new season.

tasks

FOR THE

month

Planting aquatics in baskets

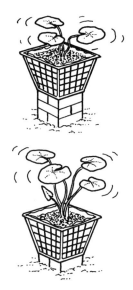

When planting aquatics lower the basket gradually into the water, removing each layer of support as the plant grows

PLANTING AQUATICS

This month and next are the main times for introducing new aquatics to the pond, because plants need to be growing actively for success. Some gardeners prefer to plant direct into a layer of soil spread evenly over the floor of the pond (see p49), but the most convenient method is to use plastic baskets, which economize both on soil and on the amount of work necessary to establish and maintain plants.

PLANTING IN BASKETS

For easy care and maintenance, water lilies and other aquatics are best grown in baskets. They prefer heavy loam containing a high proportion of stiff clay, and if your garden soil matches this requirement you can take a weedfree supply from a flower border. Lighter soil needs to be fortified with chopped turf, although it is often better to buy a proprietary planting compost for filling the baskets. You can fill them straight away if the sides are made of fine mesh, but the soil tends to wash out of larger holes and to prevent this it is a good idea to line wide-mesh baskets with hessian sacking or woven plastic. Position the rootstock so the growing tip is just above the soil surface and plant very firmly, if necessary

ramming the soil well down around the plant. Finish with a 1–2cm (up to 1in) layer of shingle or gravel to prevent soil disturbance by fish and water movement.

Once a basket is planted up it needs careful placing in the water at the appropriate depth for the species. Water the basket thoroughly with a fine-rosed can beforehand to make sure the compost is moist throughout, otherwise air bubbles will disturb the contents as you lower the plant into the pond. Where possible, sink each basket gradually to its full depth, at first resting it on a stack of bricks so that the top of the plant is near the surface; over the next few weeks as the leaves start to float, progressively remove layers of bricks until the basket reaches the final planting depth.

The same principle applies to baskets placed further from the banks of larger ponds, if you are able to wade out comfortably to reduce the depth. Where this is not possible, baskets must be sunk to their full depth straight away, using the help

of a second person on the opposite side of the pond. Cut two pieces of thin rope that will reach easily across the pond (with a little extra to allow for the maximum depth), and thread these through the top of the basket, one on each side. Suspend the basket over the surface of the water, lower it gently into position and then free the ropes.

BUYING NEW PLANTS

When choosing new plants there are a number of qualities to check before buying.
- Reject limp, tired plants in favour of those that are bright and vigorous

Dividing overgrown water lilies

- Oxygenators are usually sold in bunches of cuttings secured with lead strips: avoid any that show signs of chafing on the stems or that sport black marks, the first signs of rotting
- Bruising, brown marks and withered roots indicate mishandling, and affected samples should be rejected
- Marginals and deep-water aquatics should be pot-grown and not floating freely in the water or drying out in pre-packed bags
- Check for insect pests, clusters of eggs or jelly on the undersides of leaves, and traces of pondweed and other undesirable plants
- Unpack new purchases as soon as possible and stand in a little water, in the shade, and plant within two days of purchase

CHECKING LEAVES FOR SNAIL EGGS

When buying plants you should always reject any that bear patches of jelly, as these may contain the eggs of undesirable snails. Plants in the pond can be checked at this time of year for similar signs. Blobs of jelly that are oval or cylindrical often contain the eggs of freshwater whelks, which are vegetarian and graze on aquatic plants, and you may choose to remove these before populations become a nuisance. The brown ram's-horn snail, however, is a valuable ally that feeds on algae, and its small flat pads of eggs can safely be left to hatch.

DIVIDE OVERGROWN WATER LILIES

Water lilies may be raised from seeds or dormant eyes (see p110) or by simple division if plants are overcrowding their containers. Remove the basket from the water and carefully lift out the lily crown – this will comprise a stout main rootstock, with several smaller roots branching from the sides. Cut the smaller roots where they join the main root or, if they are longer than about 15cm (6in) long, measure 15cm (6in) from the growing tip and cut there; dusting the cut with fungicide is a useful precaution against diseases. These prepared sideshoots may then be replanted in fresh soil or compost (see margin), while the old roots and soil are all discarded.

TROUBLE WITH 'GREEN WATER'

The water in a pond that has recently been filled or refilled will often turn as green and thick as pea soup, an indication that millions of microscopic algae are multiplying at high speed. This transformation may look alarming, but it is an inevitable stage that the pond contents need to go through to achieve the perfect chemical balance. High mineral levels – either from winter and spring rains running off the soil banks or from tapwater used to top up the pond – feed this explosive growth. (See also pp64–5)

The algae continue to multiply (and, incidentally, feed a number of beneficial pond fauna) until equilibrium is restored, but sometimes the water remains green, perhaps well into midsummer, and then it will be necessary to remedy the imbalance.

HOW TO REMEDY 'GREEN WATER'

- *Do not resort to chemicals such as potassium permanganate: these treatments may cure the symptoms by killing most of the algae, but do nothing to remedy the underlying cause. Nor should you change the water, which simply postpones achieving a balance*
- *Make sure there are plenty of submerged oxygenating plants thriving in the pond, as these help consume the excess minerals*
- *Shade the recommended area of pond surface with water lilies and other floating plants (see p49) to reduce the amount of sunlight penetrating the depths*
- *Stock the pond with a few freshwater mussels, available from most water garden suppliers – these filter huge amounts of water continuously, which helps remove some of the algae*
- *Add a small amount of natural pond or stream water to the pond to introduce water fleas and other small fauna which feed on the algae*

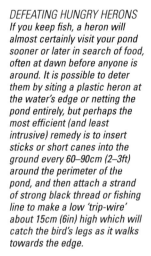

DEFEATING HUNGRY HERONS
If you keep fish, a heron will almost certainly visit your pond sooner or later in search of food, often at dawn before anyone is around. It is possible to deter them by siting a plastic heron at the water's edge or netting the pond entirely, but perhaps the most efficient (and least intrusive) remedy is to insert sticks or short canes into the ground every 60–90cm (2–3ft) around the perimeter of the pond, and then attach a strand of strong black thread or fishing line to make a low 'trip-wire' about 15cm (6in) high which will catch the bird's legs as it walks towards the edge.

WATCH OUT FOR
The evening dances of massed mayflies
The mayfly or spinner (Ephemera species) emerges from the pond this month after a lifetime burrowing as a nymph in the bottom mud. The adult flies hatch above the surface and then survive for just a few days. They are seen most spectacularly on warm still evenings, dancing and fluttering in swarms of males, all intent on attracting females and mating with them in mid-air before their brief lives come to an end.

plants
OF THE
month
1

BOG ARUM
(Calla palustris)

A wonderfully obliging plant for concealing the edge of a pond, its strong stout rhizomes gradually colonizing the shallows and supporting a lush dense carpet of handsome leaves. The autumn berries are even more attractive than the spring flowers.

type	Hardy herbaceous perennial; marginal and shallow water aquatic
flowers	Tiny and yellowish green, studded on a cylindrical spike enclosed by a prominent white funnel-shaped spathe in late spring and early summer, followed in late summer by clusters of bright red berries
foliage	Thick and heart-shaped, glossy rich green growing from strong creeping rhizomes
height	15–30cm (6–12in)
spread	30cm (12in)
position	Full sun or light shade; in very wet soil or still water, depth 0–15cm (0–6in)
planting	Spring, placing pieces of the rhizomes 23cm (9in) apart direct into wet soil or in baskets
care	Cut back dead foliage in late autumn, and divide larger clumps after 4–5 years
propagation	Division of rhizomes in early spring, either transplanted direct or started into growth in trays of mud under glass; berries (poisonous) sown when ripe in pots of wet soil
related plants	*C. aethiopica*, now *Zantedeschia aethiopica* (see p116)

◀ GLOBE FLOWER
(Trollius europaeus)

Although there are many garden hybrids, the plain species has the most charm, especially in wild gardens. Plants are non-invasive, but look most effective grown in bold drifts as this naturally occurs in large colonies.

type	Hardy herbaceous perennial; bog plant
flowers	Bright and showy golden yellow globe-shaped flowers on wiry stems; late spring and early summer
foliage	Deep green, divided and ferny like a buttercup
height	45–75cm (18–30in)

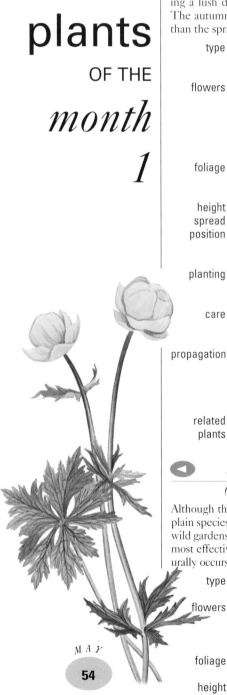

spread	30–45cm (12–18in)
position	Full sun or light shade, in damp or wet soil, or among rocks
planting	Spring or autumn, 23cm (9in) apart, in groups
care	Mulch with compost in spring, and deadhead to encourage a second flush of late flowers. Divide every 3–4 years

Bog arum

Bog bean

propagation	Division in spring or autumn; seeds sown in spring under glass
related plants	Many garden forms, grouped under *T. × cultorum*, include 'Alabaster' (cream), 'Canary Bird', 'Fire Globe' (orange), 'Golden Cup' and 'Orange Princess'; *T. chinensis*, especially 'Golden Queen' is taller and later flowering; *T. pumilus* is more dwarf, only 15cm (6in) high; *T. yunnanensis* has open orange blooms

BOG BEAN, MARSH TREFOIL
(Menyanthes trifoliata)

Another perfect marginal for planting at the water's edge for disguising the sides of a pond, although the creeping roots will also float to make large colonies in deeper water where the charming flowers look especially graceful.

type	Hardy herbaceous perennial; marginal and shallow water aquatic
flowers	White or pinkish white and star-shaped, prettily fringed in open heads; mid-spring to early summer
foliage	Smooth, shiny and bright green, divided into three pointed oval leaflets, arising from creeping rhizomes
height	23–30cm (9–12in)
spread	30–50cm (12–20in)
position	Full sun or partial shade, in very moist soil (preferably acid) or water, depth 0–30cm (0–12in)
planting	Spring, either direct into wet soil or the pond bottom, 30cm (12in) apart, or in baskets
care	Cut down dead stems in late autumn, and divide larger clumps every 4–5 years
propagation	Division in spring, cutting creeping rhizomes into several rooted sections; seeds sown in pots of wet soil in late summer

ORNAMENTAL RHUBARB
(Rheum palmatum) ▶

Second only to gunnera (p117) in size, all forms except 'Ace of Hearts' need plenty of room if they are not to look cramped. Spectacular when seen reflected in a large brooding pool.

type	Hardy herbaceous perennial; bog plant
flowers	Small, red or purple, in large plumes on stout purplish stalks up to 3m (10ft) tall; late spring and early summer
foliage	Rich green and red beneath, or reddish purple, deeply lobed and up to 90cm (3ft) across

height	1.8m (6ft)
spread	1.5–2.1m (5–7ft)
position	Full sun or semi-shade; moist rich soil as a specimen plant beside larger ponds or running water
planting	Spring, in well-prepared and richly composted soil
care	Cover dormant crowns in late autumn with leaves, bracken or garden compost, and feed with general fertilizer in spring. Either cut down faded flowerheads or leave until all topgrowth is cleared in late autumn. Divide every 4–5 years
propagation	Divide crowns with a sharp spade or axe in spring
related plants	'Atrosanguineum' has red leaved inspring and red flowers; 'Bowles' Crimson' is even deeper red; var. *tanguticum* has very deeply cut leaves; *Rheum* 'Ace of Hearts' (syn. 'Ace of Spades') is a miniature version with pink flowers

practical project 1

A POND FOR WILDLIFE

CALCULATING LINER SIZE

- Measure the greatest length (L) and width (W) of the pond
- Add to each dimension double the maximum depth (D)
- Also add 45cm (18in) for the edging overlap on both sides
- The size you need will then be L + 2D + 90cm (36in) long, by W + 2D + 90cm (36in) wide

Wildlife or natural ponds need relatively little attention once established, but careful preliminary thought and planning are vital if they are to become successful habitats. Natural ponds differ from other kinds of water garden because attracting and supporting a diverse wildlife population is their main purpose, rather than an incidental bonus, and so creating ideal surroundings is a high priority. Food, shelter, breeding and nesting sites, easy access but also cover for protection are all important design considerations, as is the choice of appropriate native plants (see p96).

On the other hand, criteria such as ornamental balance or stocking densities are less relevant because a wildlife pond tries to mirror nature rather than artistic artifice. It is not so critical if water levels fall in summer for example, because indigenous creatures are usually adapted to seasonal change, while an otherwise invasive plant species can often provide valuable cover to protect and encourage the native fauna. It is possible to adapt an existing formal pool by softening its angular lines, adding marginal steps for access and replacing exotic species with native plants, but this is rarely as successful as a purpose-built, natural pond.

Choose a site that suits the needs of wildlife for undisturbed seclusion, avoiding very shady spots that rarely attract wild creatures. Size is not critical – even a tiny pond will support newts and many small water creatures – but the larger it is, the more varied and exciting its population will become. Aim for a simple, rounded irregular shape that follows the natural contours of the ground; if you can include running or gently cascading water the extra oxygen this provides will support more active aquatic life.

●

CONSTRUCTING A WILDLIFE POND

Puddled clay (see p69) is perhaps the most natural material, but the easiest to obtain and install is a flexible liner such as butyl rubber or thick polythene sheeting (see p17). This may be covered with a layer of soil for planting directly in the pond floor, or you can arrange soil-filled hollows for this or confine plants to baskets.

- Mark the outline of the pond with a length of hosepipe, and then excavate the site and check the levels (see pp24–25). If you intend to cover the liner with soil, make the hole about 10cm (4in) and 20cm (8in) wider all round.

- Remove a strip of turf or soil around the edge of the pond, about 8cm (3in) deep and 45cm (18in) wide, to bed the edge of the liner. Clear away any sharp stones or sticks, and then line the hole with a layer of newspapers, soft sand 2.5cm (1in) thick or special fleece matting to make a smooth bed. Make sure the liner is large enough (see margin) and lay it in the excavation.

- If you are covering the liner with soil, you should mould it to the contours of the hole and smooth out any wrinkles before spreading a 10cm (4in) depth of soil over the floor and part way up the sides. Arrange pebbles and stones to create a beach area before trickling in water gently until the pond is full.

- Alternatively, stretch the liner slightly and anchor the overlap all round the edge with heavy stones or paving slabs. Running water into the pond will stretch the liner, moulding it to conform to the profile of the hole – you might need to adjust the stones wherever the liner becomes too taut.

- When the pond is full, trim the excess liner all round to leave a 45cm (18in) overlap, which can then be covered with a permanent edging.

DESIGN CRITERIA

- Shallow-sided profiles warm quickly and allow access for amphibians and birds
- A central area at least 90cm (36in) deep helps stabilize temperatures
- A pebble beach shelving into shallow water permits easy access
- Gently sloping turf is less intrusive than synthetic materials
- A rockery area can offer seclusion for hibernating frogs
- A promontory on one side or a central island is an ideal refuge for birds
- Large clumps of marginal and bog plants offer cover for amphibians from predators
- Avoid building the pond near trees that shed leaves in the water and block the flight access of water birds
- Construct a stone or timber platform for observing or feeding the wildlife
- Do not plan to stock ornamental fish as these can suppress the pond's insect life
- Allow room for at least one bog garden area as an extension to the pond

practical project 1

A POND FOR WILDLIFE

continued

A VIEWING PLATFORM

There is always something happening in an established wildlife pond, and it is a good idea to build a platform or ledge where you can quietly watch the various activities. Two or three flagstones at the water's edge (see p33) make a simple observation platform and also allow access for cleaning sessions. A small 'jetty' made of timber decking on strong supports, bedded in concrete blocks and charred or treated with preservative, is a more elaborate structure that can project over the water in larger ponds. Stepping stones or a timber footbridge (see p106) leading to a central island are other possibilities.

LAYING A PEBBLE BEACH

For a beach area to remain stable and offer wildlife easy passage to and from the pond, the slope should dip very gently into the water, and if the gradient if more than about 20° (1:5) from the horizontal, pebbles will tend to migrate downhill into the water. Bed the pebbles deeply in a 5cm (2in) layer of sand to discourage this, grading them in a natural series from the largest, up to 30cm (12in) across, at the rim of the pond to about 5cm (12in) diameter at the lower edge below water. One or two large stones set among the small pebble will look authentic, and gaps can be filled with a mix of tiny pebbles and coarse grit.

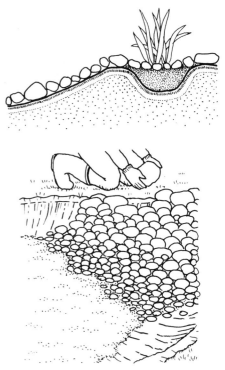

A pebble beach should slope gently down to the water. Use one or two large stones among the small pebbles to look authentic and fill gaps with tiny pebbles or grit

TURF EDGES

Edging a wildlife pond with turf enhances its natural appearance and can also provide continuity with the rest of the garden. But

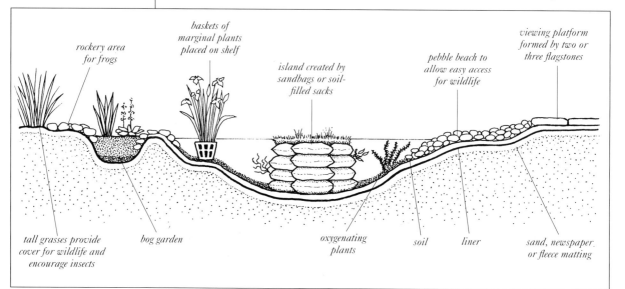

rockery area for frogs

baskets of marginal plants placed on shelf

island created by sandbags or soil-filled sacks

pebble beach to allow easy access for wildlife

viewing platform formed by two or three flagstones

tall grasses provide cover for wildlife and encourage insects

bog garden

oxygenating plants

soil

liner

sand, newspaper or fleece matting

remember that wet grass may be slippery, so only use turf edging where the pond margins are shallow. Simply relay the turves lifted during excavation so that they butt tightly together and cover the liner overlap right to the edge of the water, When mowing try to prevent clippings from falling into the pond and fouling the water, and never use lawn fertilizers, herbicides or fungicides where they might drain into the water and injure plants or wildlife.

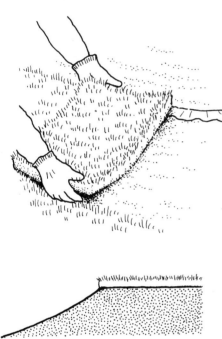

Re-lay turves lifted duing excavation to make a turf edge. They should overlap the liner edges, to the edge of the water

CREATING AN ISLAND

An ornamental highlight in any pond, an island is particularly suitable for wildlife as it offers sanctuary from predators and human disturbance. In a very large pond you can leave an area unexcavated and tailor the liner around it, but it is often easier to build an island on top of the liner after installation and before filling with water. The most appropriate size is about one-eighth to one-sixth of the pond's overall surface area. You can construct the sides of the island with sandbags or woven sacks filled with soil, or build them with rocks mortared together to

prevent soil from filtering out. Fill the island's centre with soil, or rubble topped with 15–20cm (6–8in) of ordinary garden soil. This may then be turfed, left to develop its own cover, or you can plant a few suitable native species before the pond is filled.

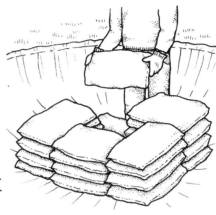

Making an island look natural
- Stop building a short distance below the final water level, and cover the top of the stack with a layer of thick turves to raise the finished surface out of the water.

- Alternatively, continue building until the sacks are just exposed above the waterline and then punch holes in them to insert young native plants for natural cover (these may also be planted in the joints between turves.)

- The final layer of sacks can be slightly inset from the sides to leave a planting shelf all round for shallow marginals.

- If the lower sacks need disguise, plant bundles of cuttings from submerged plants (see p49) in holes punched in the material.

PLANTS FOR ISLANDS

For the surface wither sow a damp ground seed mixture in cell trays for transplanting, or plant some of the following wildflowers:

Common comfrey (*Symphytum officinale*)
Cuckoo flower (*Cardamine pratensis, p46*)
Devil's bit scabious (*Succisa pratensis*)
Globe flower (*Trollius europaeus, p54*)
Grass of Parnassus (*Parnassia palustrus*)
Hemp agrimony (*Eupatorium cannabinum, p108*)
Lesser spearwort (*Ranunculus flammula, p85*)
Meadowsweet (*Filipendula ulmaria, p60*)
Purple loosestrife (*Lythrum salicaria, p84*)
Summer snowflake (*Leucojum aestivum, p35*)

PLANTS FOR EDGING

Brooklime (*Veronica beccabunga, p66*)
Bugle (*Ajuga reptans, p34*)
Cottongrass (*Eriophorum angustifolium. p67*)
Marsh marigold (*Caltha palustris, p42*)
Monkey flower (*Mimulus luteus, p108*)
Water forget-me-not (*Myosotis scorpioides, p43*)
Water mint (*Mentha aquatica, p96*)
Yellow archangel (*Lamiastrum galeobdolon*)

plants
OF THE
month
2

▼ MEADOWSWEET
(Filipendula ulmaria)

A lush and long-lived perennial for any moist position. The foliage alone would be irresistible, the leaves fresh and handsome, but the froth of sweet scented flowers adds the seductive fragrance of summer meadows.

type	Hardy herbaceous perennial; bog plant
flowers	Tiny, creamy white and perfumed, in large sprays at the tops of stems; early summer to early autumn
foliage	Deeply cut and ferny, rich green or gold, on branching stems
height	Up to 1.5m (5ft)
spread	90cm (3ft)
position	Full sun or semi-shade, in fairly rich, moist or damp soil
planting	Autumn or spring, 60cm (2ft) apart
care	Mulch in spring and feed with a general fertilizer; cut down all topgrowth in late autumn
propagation	Division of creeping rhizomes in winter or early spring; seeds sown in autumn in gentle warmth under glass
related plants	'Aurea' has golden foliage (for shade only), 'Flore Pleno' is double-flowered; *F. palmata*, 90cm (3ft), and *F. rubra* 'Magnifica', 1.8m (6ft), both have pink flowers; *F. vulgaris* (Dropwort) is like a miniature meadowsweet, 60cm (2ft) high

Houttuynia cordata

H. cordata '*Chameleon*'

▲ HOUTTUYNIA
(Houttuynia cordata)

Vigorous and easily grown, this makes attractive ground cover in any moist soil. It can become charmingly invasive unless confined in some way where neighbouring plants are at risk.

type	Hardy herbaceous or semi-evergreen perennial; bog and marginal plant
flowers	Small, white and four-petalled, each with a prominent central cone; early summer
foliage	Bold, oval or heart-shaped, blue-green or variegated, more or less evergreen
height	30cm (12in)
spread	45cm (18in)
position	Full sun or (best) partial shade, in moist or wet soil or in shallow water, depth 0–10cm (0–4in)
planting	Spring, direct into the soil or in baskets to restrain spread
care	An undemanding plant. Tidy up any faded leaves in autumn and mulch bog garden plants with compost to protect their roots from frost
propagation	Division in spring
related plants	'Flore Pleno' is double-flowered, and the popular 'Chameleon' has pink, yellow, green and white variegated leaves

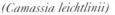

Geum rivale 'Album'

▲ WATER AVENS
(Geum rivale)

A wild plant of marshes and streamsides, closely related to the familiar garden geums but with dainty flowers, like nodding pinkish purple bells that blend well with candelabra primulas and hostas.

type	Hardy herbaceous perennial; bog plant
flowers	Small and pendent in loose heads, on arching hairy stalks; late spring to mid-summer
foliage	Rich green, rounded or lyre-shaped and irregularly toothed at the edges
height	30–45cm (12–18in)
spread	45cm (18in)
position	Semi- or light shade, although tolerates full sun, in moist soil
planting	Autumn or spring, in moist well-manured or composted and cultivated soil, 30cm (12in) apart
care	Mulch in autumn with garden compost or decayed manure, and feed in spring with general fertilizer. Cut down topgrowth in late autumn and divide clumps every 3–4 years
propagation	Division in autumn or spring
related plants	Cultivated forms include 'Album' (white), 'Dingle Apricot', 'Leonard's Variety' (pinkish orange), 'Lionel Cox' (golden yellow) and 'Variegatum'

QUAMASH ▶
(Camassia leichtlinii)

These lovely North American bulbs thrive in wet soil, yet are seldom seen in bog gardens. They are ideal for planting in wilder areas, especially under trees, where they make bold patches of colour in summer.

type	Hardy bulb; bog plant
flowers	Starry six-petalled blooms, normally blue and 4cm (1¹/₂in) across, in masses on tall stiff spikes; early and mid-summer
foliage	Long, strap-like and pointed in basal clumps
height	90cm (3ft)
spread	30cm (12in)
position	Full sun or light shade, in moist (not water-logged) areas of bog gardens and beside wildlife ponds
planting	Early to mid-autumn, 10cm (4in) deep and 15cm (6in) apart, in generous groups or drifts
care	Best left undisturbed to multiply slowly into large clumps. Water in very dry weather
propagation	Divide overcrowded clumps in autumn and replant immediately
related plants	Selections include 'Alba', 'Electra' (large, blue), 'Semiplena' (semi-double); *C. cusickii* is earlier flowering and pale blue, *C. quamash* (syn. *C. esculenta*) is white, blue or purple with shorter spikes

J U N E

The appeal of a garden pond is at its most seductive this season, and you will find yourself drawn frequently to its secret and beguiling world. A pond is made to sit by and watch, providing both a physical oasis in the garden and also a focus for tranquil contemplation: it is impossible not to relax and feel refreshed beside a pond in summer, and enjoyment is the main task of the month now.

Water lilies come into their full glory. Their thick leaves have unrolled and expanded over the surface in overlapping clusters of shining pads, covering large areas of the surface providing shade for fish and helping restrain the growth of algae. The four dark sepals enclosing each fat bud split apart to reveal the tightly furled petals that open in the sunlight into the full loveliness of the cup- or star-shaped blooms – long-lasting and often fragrant, in some varieties appearing to float on the water as though stemless, while others are held proudly well above the surface.

Since distant historical times water lilies have been admired and even worshipped. The Egyptian lotus (Nymphaea coerulea), for example, was a dynastic symbol of the early Pharaohs, while another blue lily, N. stellata, was sacred to Buddha throughout the Far East. The Greeks linked white water lilies mythologically with water nymphs, minor deities that were revered, appropriately, for their beauty and lack of solemnity, qualities these joyful flowers share in full measure. It is apt that one old-fashioned common name for the queen of aquatic plants is 'water nymph'.

CHECKLIST

- Finish planting or replanting ponds this month
- Check for signs of aphids and other plant pests
- Control blanketweed in the water
- Provide an escape route for young frogs

tasks

FOR THE

month

OTHER SEASONAL TASKS

As temperatures improve and day length increases, it is a good idea to make regular inspections to check that all is well in and around your pond

- Monitor the water level regularly and top up to compensate for any evaporation loss
- Once pond flora and fauna are fully active, you should be able to reduce or stop feeding fish
- Inspect plants for yellow leaves or poor growth, possible signs of iron or nutrient deficiency
- Test if the water temperature has reached 15°C (60°F) and then reintroduce tropical fish from indoor tanks
- If fish have spawned, make sure the fry have access to a shallow area, safe from the attentions of adult fish (see p90)
- Remove dead heads from early flowers where these are likely to fall into the water

INTRODUCING THE LAST PLANTS

Planting up ponds is a job that spreads over three or four months, starting in spring with the dormant bog garden perennials and evergreen shrubs, and ending this month with tender and tropical plants that can safely be exposed to the open air, now that soil, water and air temperatures are fairly stable.

Frost-shy subjects such as lotus, papyrus and *Pistia,* overwintered under glass in cold gardens, may now be returned to the water, together with the last species to revive: *Azolla, Lemna* and *Sagittaria,* for example. They should all be growing actively by now and will transplant successfully in this condition. Where pond construction was not started until the spring, however, the water environment may not yet be suitable for new samples of these plants, and it will then be necessary to keep them going in trays or tanks of water in the greenhouse until the pond has settled down in late summer. The plants will not suffer, but might be more difficult to handle later in the season and perhaps need cutting back before introduction to the pond. Slightly tender bulbs, such as cannas, arums and agapanthus, can also be planted out safely now. Where possible, complete all this work by the end of the month.

INSECTS AND WATER PLANTS

Once you have created a pond, insects of all kinds will inevitably arrive and take up residence. This is part of the natural evolution of a pond habitat, but unfortunately most of these species at some stage or other feed on the plants you have carefully chosen and introduced. A balanced population of pond fauna can usually prevent anything getting out of hand, but sometimes previously acceptable numbers start multiplying into an alarming invasion and then some kind of remedial treatment becomes necessary.

Aphids

Aphids can be a problem from late spring or early summer onwards, especially on water lilies, a serious infestation sometimes covering their flowers, flower stalks and leaves. Growth is often checked or distorted, but the main concern is that aphids are regular transmitters ('vectors') of a number of diseases from ailing plants to those so far unaffected. Using an insecticide to control aphid numbers (or any other insect pest for that matter) is not advisable in this context because sprays and residues ultimately enter the water where they could affect other species. The best treatment is forceful spraying with water from a hosepipe: this washes the aphids into the pond,

where fish and other predators will eat many of them. The lily aphid overwinters in plum and cherry trees; if you have any of these in the garden it is worth spraying with a winter wash to reduce dormant populations before they start returning to the pond. Remember to cover green plants around the tree with plastic before spraying and do not spray trees at the pond's edge as tar oil wash is toxic.

Other pests

Other potentially serious pests include the water lily beetle, whose larvae hatch from early summer onwards and feed on the surface tissues of the leaves. Again, forceful spraying with a jet of water is one solution; another is to cut back the foliage of marginal plants in autumn, because the adult beetles hibernate here over winter. Some midge species attack water lilies and water hawthorn, mining the leaves and skeletonizing tissues — they are rarely serious pests, which is fortunate because complete treatment is difficult, although a strong hosing with water can be partially effective.

THINNING BLANKETWEED

In addition to causing 'green water' (see p53), high levels of mineral salts in the water can produce dense mats of filamentous algae, hair-like strands that collect together to form blanketweed (also called silkweed or flannelweed). This is normally present in any healthy pond, growing on the sides and the stems of plants, where it is kept under control by grazing snails and fish. Increased sunlight at this time of year may combine with dissolved minerals to produce an explosion of growth, however, forming a thick blanket over the surface that will need to be controlled until

mineral levels subside. Chemical treatments are sometimes recommended, but the safest and easiest method is to remove large amounts manually, either drawing the fibres within reach with a garden rake or simply twisting a rough stick in the mats to wind up masses of the algae. Alternatively, try the 'straw bale

method'. Sink a bale of straw, wrapped in hessian sacking, in the pond and weight it down. When the blanket weed becomes a problem, haul out the straw bale and the weed will come with it.
Check you have not fished out any useful water creatures, and then add the blanketweed to the compost heap.

HELPING FROGS ESCAPE

Steep-sided ponds that have contained frog- or toad-spawn can pose difficulties for tadpoles as they start to turn into young adults and try to leave the water. When constructing a pond that you intend to stock with spawn, make sure part of the margin is gently sloping for easy access and escape. A sandy or pebbly beach area is another useful and attractive option, but where there is an existing steep-sided pond you can provide a suitable means of escape by partly submerging a rough board or a few logs to create a sloping ramp.

THE TROUBLE WITH DUCKWEED

Lemna trisulca, *the ivy-leafed duckweed (see p120, illus above), is a lovely little floating plant for garden pools, but some of its relatives are less restrained. They are liable to arrive, despite all your precautions – on the feet of visiting birds, for example, or tucked in the roots of bought aquatics – and once introduced, L. minor (common duckweed) and other similar species will set about rapidly dominating the pond surface. They provide useful fish spawning grounds and are liked by waterfowl, but once they start covering the water surface you should use a net regularly to thin out their numbers.*

Common duckweed

Gibbous duckweed

Great duckweed

AQUATIC ANIMALS AT THE POND SURFACE

The water will be seething with creatures by now, and many of them need a regular supply of air to survive. Watch carefully and you could see any of these.

Mosquito larvae rising and sinking as they take in air through special breathing tubes

Great pond snails crawling to the surface to fill their shells with air

A water boatman hanging from the surface film and breathing through the tip of its abdomen

Silver water beetles using the water-repellent hairs on their undersides to catch a film of air

Diving beetles, which trap bubbles of air beneath their wing cases before sinking again

Water spiders gleaming with the silvery layer of air which they take down to their underwater homes

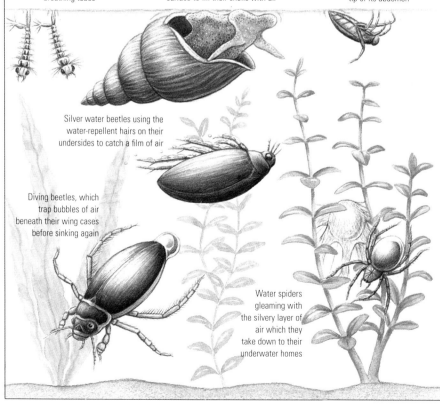

plants
OF THE
month
1

BROOKLIME
(Veronica beccabunga)

Slightly untidy but essential for the well-stocked wild garden, it is a native of shallow streams where its bright little flowers are a joy all summer.

type	Hardy herbaceous or semi-evergreen perennial; marginal and shallow water aquatic
flowers	Small, bright blue with white eyes, in clusters from leaf axils, late spring to early autumn
foliage	Glossy, oval and olive-green on long sprawling stems; deciduous in soil, evergreen below water
height	15cm (6in)
spread	45cm (18in)
position	Full sun or semi-shade, in wet soil or water, depth 0–20cm (0–8in)
planting	Spring, 30cm (12in) apart, direct in the soil or in baskets to restrain them
care	Undemanding once established. Trim back stems if they become invasive or untidy; horizontal stems root readily as runners wherever they touch the ground
propagation	Seeds sown in a cold frame in spring; tip cuttings in summer rooted straight into the ground; division in spring; separation of rooted runners any time

ARROW ARUM
(Peltandra undulata, syn. *P. virginica)*

With typical white or greenish spathes, this is more suited to larger ponds as it is quite tall and spreading.

type	Hardy semi-evergreen perennial; marginal and shallow water aquatic
flowers	Tiny, on a short spike enclosed by a conspicuous greenish white spathe, in early summer, followed by green berries
foliage	Rich green, shiny and arrow-shaped, evergreen in deeper water
height	60cm (2ft)
spread	45cm (18in)
position	Full sun or light shade, at the edge of medium-size or large ponds, or in water, depth 0–25cm (0–10in)
planting	Spring, 30cm (12in) apart, in natural groups, direct into the soil
care	Remove any dead foliage in winter
propagation	Division of creeping rhizomes in spring
related plants	*P. sagittifolia*, syn. *P. alba* (White Arrow Arum) is a purer white with red berries

DAY LILY
(Hemerocallis cultivars)

Day lilies (and each individual flower *does* last only a day) are grown all over the garden, but thrive best in fairly moist soil, which makes them flamboyant additions to bog gardens.

type	Hardy herbaceous perennial; bog plant
flowers	Large, brightly coloured trumpets, in continuous succession from early to late summer
foliage	Narrow, arching and strap-like, in strong clumps
height	45cm–1.2m (18–48in)
spread	45–60cm (18–24in)
position	Full sun, in rich moist soil, in groups or combined with irises, best where the foliage is reflected in still water
planting	Autumn or spring, 45–60cm (18–24in) apart, in soil well enriched with compost or decayed manure
care	Mulch in autumn with compost and feed in spring with a general fertilizer. Cut down all growth in late winter. Divide vigorous varieties every 2 years, other kinds after 3–5 years
propagation	Division in autumn or spring
related plants	Numerous cultivars such as 'Anzac' (red), 'Black Magic' (purple), 'Golden Chimes', 'Hyperion' (yellow), 'Luxury Lace' (lavender), 'Pink Damask' and

'Stella de Oro' (dwarf yellow); *H. citrina* and *H. lilioasphodelus* are charming, fragrant yellow species

RODGERSIA

(Rodgersia tabularis, syn. Astilboides tabularis)

Superb foliage plant whose enormous leaves can carpet a large area of shaded soil. Majestic plumes of flowers erupt in summer, and look stunning in groups beside larger stretches of still water.

type	Hardy evergreen perennial; bog plant
flowers	Small, white or pinkish white, in large panicles on stout branching stalks in mid-summer, followed by red seedheads
foliage	Large, up to 50cm (20in) wide, lobed and crinkled
height	Up to 1.5m (5ft)
spread	75cm (30in)
position	Partial or light shade, in rich moist soil, beside large ponds
planting	Autumn or spring, in rich soil fortified with plenty of compost or leafmould
care	Mulch in autumn with garden compost and feed with a general fertilizer in spring. Leave seedheads until winter before cutting
propagation	Seeds sown in autumn in a cold frame; division in autumn or spring
related plants	*R. aesculifolia* has bronze-green leaves like a horse-chestnut; *R. pinnata* is smaller with pointed leaves, and *R. p.* 'Superba' is pink-flowered; *R. podophylla* has palmate leaves, purple in the form 'Rotlaub'

COTTON GRASS

(Eriophorum angustifolium)

An elegant, slow-growing grass, native to high-altitude marches and moorlands with acid soils, it is quite unmistakable in late summer when its seedheads form cottonwool-like tufts.

type	Hardy perennial grass; bog and marginal plant
flowers	Small with bright yellow anthers, in early to mid-spring, followed in summer by brown seedpods enclosing tufts of white silky hairs
foliage	Dark green, long, slim and drooping, in clumps
height	45–75cm (18–30in)
spread	30cm (12in)
position	Full sun or semi-shade, in wet peaty acid soil or in shallow water, depth 0–10cm (0–4in)
planting	Spring, 23cm (9in) apart
care	Undemanding provided it has acid soil and water. Mulch in spring if soil is likely to dry out, and feed with a general fertilizer in spring while young
propagation	Seeds sown in wet ericaceous compost under glass in spring; division in spring
related plants	*E. latifolium* (Broad-leafed Cotton Grass) is similar and tolerates lime

practical project 1

MAKING A BOG GARDEN

THE WEED PROBLEM
Bog garden plants naturally grow vigorously and soon cover the ground, suppressing the germination of annual weeds. Perennial weed species, however, may be a problem, especially as hoeing is difficult in wet soil and spraying with herbicides is inadvisable near a pond. When preparing the site for a bog garden, therefore, search the soil thoroughly for fragments of weed roots to make as clean a start as possible. Other precautions include spraying the site with systemic herbicide once or twice before starting excavation, and leaving the prepared bed fallow for several weeks so that overlooked weeds can grow and be removed before planting begins.

A bog garden or marsh garden is a specialized place for growing those plants that like wet conditions. Some marginal species will flourish here, together with many familiar garden plants that need plenty of moisture but which cannot tolerate being waterlogged for long periods.

Sometimes a suitable bog garden site occurs naturally, perhaps where the water table approaches the surface or in a low lying depression where a stream regularly floods its banks, but these habitats are subject to fluctuating moisture levels and can dry out disastrously in summer. Bog plants need a consistent environment, and it is usually best to create a special site using materials that ensure stability.

The most appropriate position is immediately adjacent to a garden pond, so that the plants blend with others of similar habitats and the soil moisture content can be regulated closely; the simplest way to construct such a bed is as an overflow garden, the first method below. There is no reason, however, why a bog garden may not be sited further away or even succeed as a feature in its own right in an otherwise conventional garden, and either the irrigated or hydroponic arrangement would be suitable here.

AN OVERFLOW BOG GARDEN

Immediately next to an existing pond or the cavity for a new one, excavate the bog garden site at least 30cm (12in) deep, making sure you leave a strong wall of soil still enclosing the pond but slightly lower than elsewhere so that water can overflow into the bog garden. Level the site and bank the walls gently; then break up any soil lumps, rake a fine tilth on the surface and cover this with a 5cm (2in) layer of grit or coarse sand. Spread thick polythene or pond liner over the whole area, including the adjacent pond wall, puncture the liner at 90cm (3ft) intervals with a sharp spike or knife and then cover with a further 5cm (2in) thickness of

Overflow bog garden

grit – this is to prevent the drainage holes from clogging up with soil. Finally, fill the bed with good garden soil, mixing some fibrous compost in to extremely light or heavy soil as a conditioner and, if possible, spreading a base layer of well-rotted manure over the grit to help retain moisture. Surplus water from rainfall or from topping up the pond will spill into the bed and keep it moist, although you might have to run water in regularly during a dry summer.

AN IRRIGATED BOG GARDEN

This is constructed in a similar way, but do not puncture the liner. Spread a 5–8cm (2–3in) layer of grit on top, burying within this one or more parallel lengths of perforated plastic pipe, stopped at the far end and connected at the other end to a cistern or hosepipe coupling; space multiple pipes about 1.8m (6ft) apart. Cover the grit with a sheet of woven plastic matting to prevent soil from clogging the irrigation pipe, and then fill the bed with soil as above.

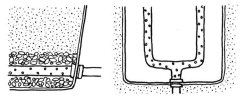

Pipe system for an irrigated bog garden

A HYDROPONIC BOG GARDEN

Hydroponics is the science of growing plants without soil and sustaining their growth with regular applications of liquid fertilizer, a method which can be used very effectively for constructing a bog bed anywhere in the garden. Prepare the site as described for an overflow bog garden, lining

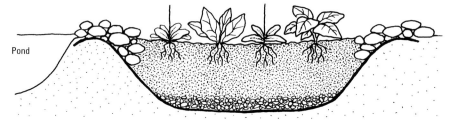

Pond

Hydroponic bog garden

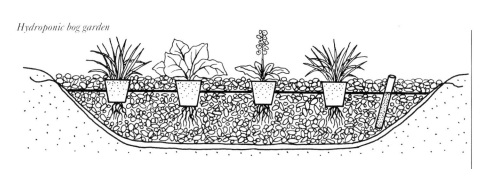

the excavation with unperforated thick polythene or pool liner and then completely filling the bed with 2–2.5cm (³/₄–1in) gravel. Close to one side, insert a length of 10cm (4in) drainpipe vertically almost to the bottom of the gravel, so that the water level can be checked and topped up at any time, and then run water from a hosepipe into the bed until it reaches about 15cm (6in) below the surface. Plants need large rootballs to thrive in this kind of bed, so choose specimens grown in 15–20cm (6–8in) pots or standard 3–5 litre containers and plant them in the same way as in a conventional border. Water individually every 10–14 days with a solution of liquid fertilizer, and check the water level regularly, although even in summer there will be less evaporation than you might expect.

A DAMP WILDFLOWER MEADOW

The appearance and diversity of a wildlife pond will be enhanced by a wildflower bog garden. Prepare the site in the usual way and refill the bed with the excavated soil – do not add fertilizers or soil conditioners as these affect wildflower growth. Sow the bed with a mixture of native species, raking the seeds gently into the surface. Prepared wet meadow mixtures can be bought, or you can blend your own with species such as bird's foot trefoil, buttercup, cowslip, oxeye daisy, ragged robin, devil's-bit scabious, yellow rattle and other moisture-loving species, combined with about 75% low-maintenance grasses. One annual cut after flowering will keep the meadow in good condition.

See also:
Cleaning up the bog garden, p20
Effective plant protection, p12
Mulching moist areas, p136
Planting bog garden perennials, p114
Planting the bog garden, p41
Weeding the bog garden, p76

USING PUDDLE CLAY

Perhaps the least common way of making a pond is to prepare a base of heavy clay. This is very successful in areas of naturally heavy soil, although elsewhere high quality sticky clay can be bought for the purpose. It is laid or trodden in place while wet (hence the term puddle clay) to form an impervious layer, but its efficiency is reduced if the layer is penetrated by tree roots or allowed to dry out in summer. Excellent bog gardens and even natural ponds can be made on clay ground simply by treading the dampened exposed surface of the excavation until it is very firm. Refill bog gardens with a prepared planting mixture; cover the base and shelves of ponds with 20cm (8in) of soil for planting into, or grow aquatics in baskets.

plants

OF THE

month

2

WATER LILIES

These perennial aquatic plants, with their familiar floating leaves or 'pads' and flowers of matchless beauty, are often the first choice when gardeners start planting up a pond. Selection needs care, however, for the term 'water lily' embraces two main genera, Nymphaea (Water Lily) and Nuphar (Pond Lily), superficially similar but culturally quite different. Nymphaea varieties are further divided into tropical and hardy kinds, both groups each containing lilies that can be subdivided according to size and vigour: dwarf, small, medium and large. Add to this complexity the bewildering range of colours, shapes and fragrances (the varieties listed are a very small sample), and it is clear that careful selection is important, especially if you only have room for a single variety.

HARDY WATER LILIES
(Nymphaea spp.)

These comprise the bulk of available water lilies, all of them very hardy and long-lived, but variable in size, which in turn affects their preferred planting depth. They are valuable plants, not just for their exquisite beauty but also because they shade the surface of the pond for many months, suppressing the growth of algae and offering shelter to fishes. As a rough guide, the area of surface covered is about 1½ times the planting depth.

type	Hardy herbaceous perennial; shallow or deep water aquatics
flowers	Cup- or star-shaped, in a wide range of colours that often alter with age, up to 25cm (10in) across, each floating on the surface for 3–4 days but followed by others in succession; between late spring and mid-autumn
foliage	Oval or heart-shaped, thick, shiny and mid-green, sometimes with wavy edges or attractive variegation, floating on the surface
spread	30–250cm (1–8ft)
position	Full sun, in still water, depth 10–90cm (4–36in) according to type

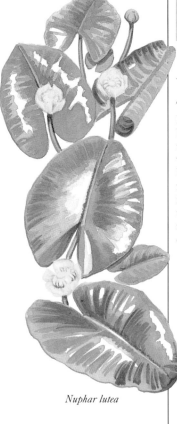

Nuphar lutea

planting	Late spring or early summer, as rhizomes or young plants, singly direct into the soil of large ponds, or in baskets, so that the tip of the rhizome is just above surface level (see p52)
care	Submerge baskets gradually over several weeks as the leaves and leaf stalks grow. Remove dead flowerheads and leaves as they fade. Divide or repot every 3–5 years
propagation	Division in spring (see p52)

TROPICAL WATER LILIES
(Nymphaea spp)

These tender tuberous plants with elegant flowers in brilliant colours, need heated greenhouse conditions and are therefore ideal for indoor ponds (see p128) or for planting out in summer in warm districts. Before the first frosts tubers of outdoor plants must be lifted and stored in water or damp sand at a minimum temperature of 5°C (41°F). Plants prefer to grow in shallow water, about 10–30cm (4–12in) deep, that will quickly warm up in sunshine. Only a small selection of day-flowering Nymphaea varieties is given here: 'Afterglow' (peach and rose), 'Blue Beauty' (dark blue), 'Colonel Lindbergh' (pale blue), 'Director George T. Moore' (dark red), 'Mrs C. W. Ward' (pale pink), 'Pamela' (pale blue), 'Pink Platter', 'Yellow Dazzler'.

HARDY POND LILIES
(Nuphar spp)

Compared with water lilies, Nuphar species such as N. lutea and N. variegata are very vigorous and invasive. Achieving enormous proportions, they are suited only to large ponds or lakes, in water 90–250cm (3–8ft) deep. Their yellow fragrant flowers are comparatively small, whereas the large foliage can cover an area of more than 1.8 x 1.8m (6 x 6ft). N. japonica var. variegata and N. pumila variegata are much smaller, thriving in a depth of 30–45cm (12–18in), and make useful additions to a wildlife pond.

HARDY WATER LILY VARIETIES

varieties	flowers	leaves
Dwarf, pygmy or miniature – planting depth 10–30cm (4–10in)		
'Aurora'	yellow to orange then red, semi-double	mottled
N. candida	white, golden stamens, bright red stigmas	
'Froebelii'	vivid red, single, prolific	olive-green
'Graziella'	copper, orange stamens, free flowering	purple-flecked
N. x helvola	pale yellow, golden centred, tiny, prolific	brown-mottled
'Laydekeri Fulgens'	crimson, red stamens, single	purple-flecked
'Laydekeri Lilacea'	rose deepening to red, single	flecked
'Odorata Minor'	white, very fragrant	red undersides
'Paul Hariot'	yellow becoming red, large, free flowering	purple-flecked
N. tetragona (syn. 'Pygmaea Alba')	smallest of all, single, white	purple-backed
Small – planting depth 15–45cm (6–18in)		
'Albatross'	white, large, single	young leaves dark red
'Commanche'	pink, yellow and orange, semi-double	purple at first
'Gloriosa'	crimson, red stamens, fragrant, semi-double	
'James Brydon' stands shade	bright red, double, fragrant	red-flecked;
'Livingstone'	red striped white, brownish centre, deep cup-shaped	
'Odorata Sulphurea Grandiflora'	yellow, semi-double	marbled and spotted
'Robinsoniana'	orange-red, light orange centres	marked purple
'Rose Nymph'	deep rose-pink, large, fragrant	
'Sioux'	buff-yellow, eventually copper-red	mottled brown
Medium – planting depth: 30–60cm (1–2ft)		
'Amabilis'	rose pink, large, flat, single	pointed
'Conqueror'	crimson, white sepals, large, semi-double	young leaves purple
'Escarboucle'	wine-red, fragrant, semi-double, very free flowering	
'Mme Wilfron Gonnère'	rich pink, rose centred, double, cup-shaped	
'Marliacea Carnea'	pale pink, darkening, large, fragrant, free flowering;	
'Moorei'	pale yellow, semi-double	brown-flecked
N. odorata	white, gold stamens, very fragrant	purple young leaves
'René Gerard'	red streaked, pink, large, semi-double free flowering;	
'Sunrise'	bright yellow, gold stamens, semi-double, fragrant	red beneath
'William Falconer'	blood-red, orange stamens	deep purple at first
Large – planting depth 45–90cm (1½–3ft)		
N. alba vigorous	white, yellow stamens, double, very large	
'Attraction'	rich garnet-red, flecked white, larger on older plants	
'Charles de Meurville'	burgundy-red, tipped white, gold stamens	large
'Colossea'	pink fading to white, very large, fragrant, semi-double	
'Gladstoneana'	white, gold centred, double, to 30cm (12in) across	
'Marliacea Chromatella'	canary yellow, tinged pink, very large	splashed with brown
'Mrs Richmond'	pink becoming red, gold stamens	pale green, wavy
N. tuberosa 'Richardsonii' needs very deep water	white, yellow stamens, semi-double	

Hardy water lilies (from top to bottom): 'Laydeckeri fulgens', 'Sunrise', N. tetragona, 'Blue Beauty', 'Gladstoneana' and 'Attraction'

practical project 2

INTRODUCING FISH TO A POND

HOW TO IDENTIFY HEALTHY FISH

Qualities to look for:
a strong upright dorsal (top) fin
well-expanded ventral (stomach) fins
bright eyes
lively behaviour

Features to avoid:
missing scales
raised white spots anywhere on the body
sluggish or excessively fast movement

It is often said that no pond is complete without a few fish, and certainly they add colour and animation to the water garden. Their role in the overall balance of pond life is limited, although they do help reduce midge and mosquito populations. It is worth noting, though, that in a wildlife pond fish may make many other inhabitants suffer as well: without control by natural predators (apart from the passing heron or cat), they stand at the top of the food chain and may clear the pond of tadpoles, dragonfly larvae and other welcome creatures. You can avoid this imbalance by dividing the pond in two, excluding the fish from the wilder section. Nonetheless, they are attractive additions to the pond community, especially in formal pools where a mixture of brightly coloured fancy fish will provide endless fascination.

CREATING THE IDEAL HABITAT

Make sure the centre of the pond is at least 45cm (18in) deep, and discuss with your dealer whether you should add filtration and aeration equipment (see p.86); this may be necessary for Koi carp whose scavenging destroys plants and muddies the water, or where high stocking rates might otherwise pollute the water with waste products.

A new pond must be allowed time to settle down before introducing fish (see margin), and a varied population of plants should be in place, including plenty of submerged oxygenating species to provide protective cover and green food. Floaters and deep water aquatics create the shade that fish need during the summer.

Remember that most fish scavenge and nose around everywhere and can disturb the soil and roots of freshly planted aquatics, so give these time to establish, and cover the soil in baskets with a thick layer of gravel for protection.

CHOOSING YOUR FISH

Stock the pond gradually, adding a few fish at a time rather than all at once, and introduce them in late spring or early summer when temperatures are more stable. Although you can buy fish by mail order, it is better to see them at a stockist and inspect their colour, shape and health for yourself (see margin). Always choose medium-size fish to avoid the problems associated with small specimens and the expense of buying adults, and make

sure your choices match the conditions in which they are to live, both in terms of stocking rate and the type of pond: there are some species, such as dace, roach and rudd, which will thrive in a wildlife environment, whereas bright, clearly visible fish are better suited to formal ponds of various sizes.

These are perhaps the most popular and readily available types:

- **Common goldfish** – the most familiar pond fish, fairly inexpensive and usually red-gold, yellow or cream in colour; they grow to 30–38cm (12–15in) long, live for 10–15 years (sometimes more) and are perfectly hardy, even in shallow water.

- **Shubunkins** – fancy cousins of the common goldfish, these have larger fins and more ornamental, graceful shapes; they are easy to keep but prefer depths over 30cm (12in) in winter, as do **Comets**, their sleeker and even more colourful relatives.

- **Fancies** – Fantails, Moors, Orandas and similar beautiful or bizarre varieties with complex shapes and colours are less hardy and really belong in an aquarium; they are very popular, however, and may be included in your pond selection provided they are overwintered indoors.

- **Golden orfe** – for larger ponds, minimum surface area about 4m² (43ft²), these slender elegant fish are great favourites; they move fast, stay near the surface and tolerate fountains and other moving water features that provide the extra oxygen they need.

- **Koi carp** – most impressive of all pond fish, these ornamental Japanese varieties can reach 90cm (3ft) in length and therefore need a very large pond with a depth of at least 1.2m (4ft); they are also vigorous scavengers, disturbing plants and muddying the water, so efficient filtration is essential.

CARING FOR YOUR FISH

Fish are generally quite self-sufficient if they live in good conditions, and supplementary feeding is the main attention they need. Well-planted ponds will supply much of their diet, but spring and summer are active seasons when they benefit from protein-rich foods given regularly (see p41); in autumn occasional supplements will help prepare them for winter.

STOCKING RATES

How many fish can live happily in your pond is calculated according to their size, and the usual rule of thumb is to allow 5cm (2in) length for every 0.09m² (approx. 1ft²). Thus a pond 1.8m² (20ft²) will comfortably hold 10 fish 10cm (4in) long or 5 fish 20cm (8in) long. Ideally, buy fish about 8–10cm (3–4in) long and allow space for their growth.

An alternative way to determine stocking rates is by weight to volume, allowing an average of 50–100g (2–4oz) of fish to every 1000 litres (220 gallons) of water in the pond.

GETTING THE WATER RIGHT

To provide the best conditions for fish, you should wait about six weeks after filling the pond. During the first fortnight fresh water will become green and then cloudy as micro-organisms start to develop. Aquatic plants can be introduced at this stage, and their activity helps to absorb dissolved minerals and produce oxygen, so that by the fifth or sixth week the water will become clear once more, which is an indication that it is safe to add your fish (see margin, Introducing Fish).

INTRODUCING FISH
Fish are sensitive to changes in temperature, so avoid any shocks when transferring them to the pond.

Float the bag in which you brought your fish home in the pond

Add some pond water to the bag and leave for 10 minutes

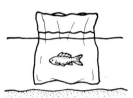

Add more pond water and leave for a further 10 minutes

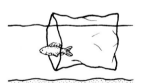

Push the bag over on its side and the fish will swim out when it is ready

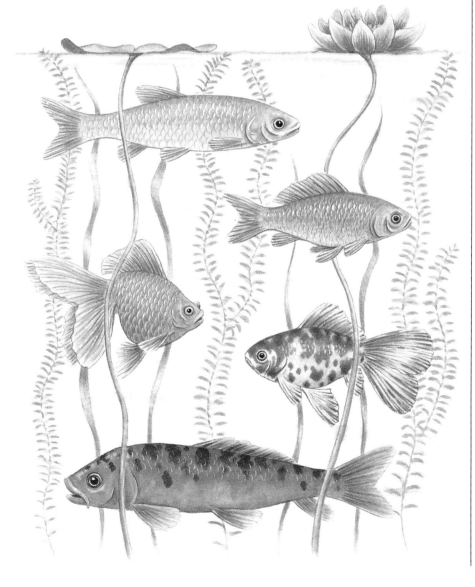

(left) A variety of popular pond fish. (from top to bottom) Golden orfe, common goldfish, shubunkin, fantail and koi carp

JULY

Most of the marginal plants are at their peak now, their stems jostling
for sunlight and their flowers fully open in the drowsy heat. Some
mature explosively, casting their seeds far out on to the pond surface
where they will slowly drift to new seed beds elsewhere. Others are less
efficient at producing seeds and are busy instead at the bottom of the
pond, their new roots and rhizomes creeping in all directions and
knitting a close mesh that traps soil particles and leaf debris to create
a deeper habitat both for themselves and for the organisms that live
and feed there.

In deeper water, oxygenators and floating aquatics can increase at an
alarming rate. They are valuable plants that provide essential food,
cover and spawning grounds for the pond fauna, and improve the
water quality by releasing oxygen and mopping up dissolved minerals
which might otherwise act as fertilizer for algae. Left unchecked in a
thriving pond, however, their vigorous growth can choke the deeper
zones, in the long term adding more organic materials to the sediment
and contributing to the slow decline of the pond, so it is important to
drag out handsful of the profuse growth several times during summer.
The matted algal filaments of blanketweed and 'green water', caused
by the rapid multiplication of minute free-swimming algae in nutrient-
rich water, are further possible problems in summer, obscuring the
water and making it impossible to see what is happening below the
surface. Keeping the water clear is essential if you want to watch the
underwater world in action.

One of the best times to explore the water depths is after dark, by
shining a torch into the pond to reveal submerged wildlife activity,
often with greater clarity than during the day. Many creatures, from
newts and great diving beetles to camouflaged caddisfly larvae and
tiny mites, can all be found busily swimming, stalking or feeding on
passing creatures at night.

CHECKLIST

- Oxygenate ponds if fish are distressed
- Deal with leeches
- Thin oxygenating plants and floaters
- Weed and water the bog garden
- Sow water lilies

tasks
FOR THE
month

*DISSOLVED OXYGEN LEVELS
The oxygen content of pond
water decreases as
temperatures rise; fish usually
start to gulp air at the surface or
leave trails of bubbly froth when
water temperatures rise above
25°C (77°F). This table indicates
the dramatic change in oxygen
content.*

Water temperature	Oxygen content
5°C (41°F)	*12.75 mg/ltr*
10°C (50°F)	*11.25 mg/ltr*
15°C (59°F)	*10 mg/ltr*
20°C (68°F)	*9 mg/ltr*
25°C (77°F)	*8.25 mg/ltr*
30°C (86°F)	*7.5 mg/ltr*

OXYGENATING THE WATER

Fish need oxygen dissolved in the pond water for their normal metabolism to work efficiently. A typical symptom of oxygen deficiency is the congregation of fish at the surface, gulping frantically for air: this is most likely to happen in a warm sultry season (see margin), in still or shallow ponds. If you install and regularly run a fountain or moving water feature, this problem should rarely occur. Agitating a jet from a hosepipe on the surface for a few minutes occasionally will often aerate the water sufficiently, but you should also check that there are not too many submerged plants for the size of pond, as these can actively compete with the fish for the available oxygen, sometimes leading to overnight casualties (see p90). Other causes may be insufficient shade cast by floating plants and marginals, large amounts of decomposing material on the pond bottom, over-population of fish, or an excess of blanketweed.

DEALING WITH LEECHES

If you keep finding intact but empty snail shells in the pond, there is a strong chance that they are the casualties of leeches, which can become a nuisance to fish too. Leeches feed through terminal suckers by which they attach themselves to their victim,

gorging on blood before letting go and hiding once more among water plants while digesting their meal. The wounds they leave behind can open the way to other, more deadly disorders. Although leeches are rarely a serious menace, if you suspect a major infestation it is possible to treat them with any of the specific preparations now available. Alternatively the traditional method is to suspend a piece of raw meat in the water on the end of a line – this usually attracts them in large numbers.

THINNING FLOATING AQUATICS

A layer of silt will build up slowly on the bottom of a

pond as plant debris sinks to the bottom and starts to decompose, combined with the bodies of various microscopic pond fauna. The formation of this is a perfectly natural part of a pond's evolution, and necessary, too, because many plants and animals depend on it for their existence. Too much silt, however, can jeopardize water quality, a risk you can help avoid by thinning invasive floating and oxygenating plants during the summer, before they reach excessive densities. Most species are simply dragged out with a net or lifted on a piece of material wrapped around the tines of a garden fork. They are ideal for composting or, if needed elsewhere, may be kept in good condition for a while in tanks of water.

WEEDING THE BOG GARDEN

No matter how careful you are when creating a bog garden (see p68), some weed fragments will survive and re-establish themselves, while others are almost certain to arrive from various sources.

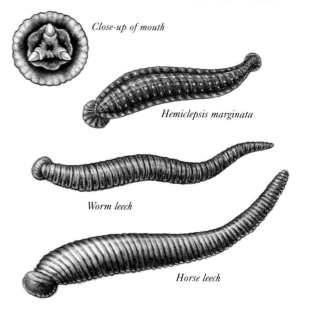

Close-up of mouth

Hemiclepsis marginata

Worm leech

Horse leech

In addition, a few plants introduced enthusiastically as desirable may have settled in too well and become invasive, so that thinning becomes necessary to prevent their overwhelming more restrained behaved plants.

Weeding a bog garden is not easy. Hoeing is impossible in mud or even moderately moist soil, and forking is seldom light rapid work when the ground is wet. For this reason, it is often a good idea to leave weeding until the summer when the ground tends to dry out regularly. Just before topping up moisture levels in the bog garden, go round and tidy up generally, forking out weeds wherever possible or chopping them out with a hoe – clear away any remains straight away, because fragments left on the surface will surely root again once the garden is watered. Remember that using weedkillers is not advisable in case residues leach into the water and affect other, more precious plants.

WATERING THE BOG GARDEN

A well-made bog garden should remain moist for much of the time, especially if designed to take surplus water from the pond after prolonged rainfall. In a warm dry season, however, this overflow may not occur and shallow bog gardens can start to dry out. If you have installed trickle irrigation below ground (see p68), it is simply a matter of turning on the water for a short while. Alternatively water the garden with a sprinkler for an evening or gently trickle water into the pond from a hosepipe until it overflows into the bog garden (but remember this can aggravate any problems with 'green water', see p53).

PROPAGATING LILY SEED

Very occasionally hybrid water lilies set seeds and it is always worth collecting any seedpods to sow the contents and see whether an interesting new variety might result. The miniature white lily, Nymphaea tetragona (see p71), regularly sets seeds and this is its normal method of propagation since the rootstock does not produce eyes (see p110).

- *The tiny seeds are embedded in jelly inside a pea-like pod, which is harvested when dark green; do not try to separate the individual seeds from the jelly*
- *Fill a pan or pot with moist, sieved potting compost or aquatic planting compost, and firm lightly*
- *Spread the contents of the seedpod evenly across the surface and thinly cover with compost*
- *Very gently set the pan in a tray of water so the compost is covered to a depth of about 2.5cm (1in), and keep in a warm place out of direct sunlight*
- *Seedlings emerge after 4–6 weeks; raise the water level gradually to keep them covered as they grow*
- *Once the first true leaves appear, seedlings can be pricked out: ease them from the compost, separate them by washing gently (they are very fragile), and space them out in pans so they do not touch; cover with water as before*
- *Pot on the young plants as they grow, keeping them covered with water, until early the following summer when they can be planted out in the pool.*

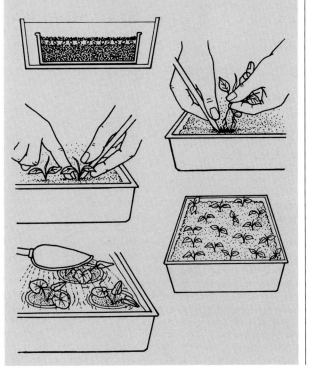

WATCH OUT FOR
The spinning whirligig beetle
This remarkably athletic creature is a small round black beetle (appropriately called Gyrinus) that lives in social groups usually found spiralling around at high speed on the pond surface. Its eyes are divided horizontally, enabling it to see above and below water simultaneously. It can dive and chase food, and lives mainly on larvae and aquatic insects, although large numbers may become a nuisance if they prey on fish fry.

plants
OF THE
month
1

FLOWERING RUSH
(Butomus umbellatus)

Not a true rush, despite its name and foliage, but a very attractive perennial flower at home beside still shallow water, and cultivated in parts of Asia for its nutritious rhizomes. The flowers dry well.

type	Hardy herbaceous perennial; marginal plant
flowers	Large and rose-pink, 2.5cm (1in) across, 20–30 clustered in upright spreading umbels on tall smooth stems; mid- and late summer
foliage	Narrow and rush-like, triangular in section, green or purplish
height	Up to 1.5m (5ft)
spread	60cm (2ft)
position	Full sun, at the edge of larger ponds, in boggy or muddy ground, or shallow water, depth 5–15cm (2–6in)
planting	Spring, 23cm (9in) apart in clumps of 5–10 plants, direct into the soil or in baskets
care	Cut down all growth in autumn. Divide every 3 years or so, before flowering vigour declines
propagation	Seeds sown under glass in autumn; division in spring; bulbils removed from the sides of rhizomes during division
related plants	The excellent white form 'Schneeweissen'

ARROWHEAD, DUCK POTATO
(Sagittaria sagittifolia, syn. *S. japonica)*

Another perennial with edible roots, also favoured by some fish and birds. The leaves are quite distinctive and, combined with the flowers of the double form, make this a desirable though rather invasive marginal for large ponds.

type	Hardy herbaceous perennial; marginal plant
flowers	Fairly large, white with black and red centres, in spikes, male flowers at the top and females below; mid- and late summer
foliage	Variable according to water depth, from long submerged ribbons to elegant, arrow-shaped leaves above the surface
height	45–60cm (18–24in)
spread	30–45cm (12–18in)
position	Full sun or light shade, at the edge of larger ponds, in shallow water, depth 5–30cm (2–12in); tolerates deeper water but flowering is depressed
planting	Spring, 23cm (9in) apart, in groups direct into the soil in large ponds, or in baskets
care	Cut back all growth in autumn. Divide and replant every 2–3 years where overcrowded
propagation	Seeds sown under glass in spring; division of clumps in spring; separation of bulb-like buds at the ends of stolons in autumn
related plants	'Flore Pleno' is attractively double-flowered; *S. latifolia* is similar but less hardy; *S. subulata* is a deep water oxygenating plant

(top) Arrowhead and (above) pickerel weed

PICKEREL WEED
(Pontederia cordata)

An uninspired common name for a glorious aquatic that is far from weedy. Sited in groups in deeper water, the plants are little trouble and come into their own when most other flowers have finished.

type	Hardy herbaceous perennial; shallow or deep water aquatic
flowers	Tiny, pale blue to purple, massed tightly on cylindrical spikes; mid-summer to early autumn
foliage	Mat rich green, spear- or heart-shaped on strong stalks rising from the water
height	Up to 75cm (30in)
spread	45cm (18in)
position	Full sun or light shade, in isolated specimen groups in medium-sized or large ponds, in water depth 10–38cm (4–15in)
planting	Spring, 30cm (12in) apart, in small groups direct into the soil, or in baskets to limit spread (more restrained in deeper water); make sure at least 8cm (3in) of water covers the crown to avoid frost damage
care	Undemanding once established. If plants are grown as marginals, protect the crowns against frost with a mulch of bracken in autumn
propagation	Seeds sown in autumn in submerged pots under glass; division in spring
related plants	The form *alba* has handsome white flowers, while var. *lancifolia* is taller with slim leaves

ASTILBE
(Astilbe × arendsii)

Many hybrid varieties are available, all of them desirable for planting in groups beside natural or wildlife ponds, where they combine well with ferns and hostas. They are also good for cutting.

type	Hardy herbaceous perennial; bog plant
flowers	Individually tiny, but gathered in great numbers in large feathery plumes, ranging from white to deep red; late spring to early autumn
foliage	Dainty, finely cut and very decorative, green with red or bronze tints
height	60–90cm (2–3ft)
spread	45cm (18in)
position	Full or semi-shade, in moist or wet soil with plenty of humus, as single or blending colours in groups
planting	Autumn or spring, 30cm (12in) apart, in groups or drifts, in soil that has been enriched with plenty of garden compost or leafmould
care	Mulch in spring with compost or decayed manure. Cover older crowns with compost if they are heaved out of the ground, and divide every 3–4 years to rejuvenate plants
propagation	Seeds (species and mixtures) sown under glass in spring; division in spring
related plants	Apart from *A. × arendsii* hybrids, try dwarf *A. × crispa*, 15–20cm (6–8in), and semi-dwarf *A. simplicifolia* forms in waterside rockeries

For centuries oriental gardens, with their unique blend of natural elements and an atmosphere of unity with nature, have exerted a powerful fascination on European gardeners. Central to most Chinese and Japanese gardening styles is an artful use of water in both its aspects – the joy and vitality of streams and flowing watercourses, and the brooding intensity of still pools that invite quiet meditation. Oriental pond features have often been borrowed and incorporated in the composition of western water garden designs, and in their different ways they translate successfully, adding a simple and natural charm that can be very satisfying.

practical project 1

DESIGNING AN ORIENTAL POND

A Chinese garden

Rocks and water are the main elements in a Chinese garden: the Chinese term *shan shui* (landscape) means 'mountains and water'. A stream or waterfall represents the vitality of life, with all its richness and variety, whereas the flat still surface of a pool is intended to reflect the sky, regarded symbolically as half the universe. The other half of the universe is represented by stones and rocks, often piled high or selected for their bizarre shapes. Decorative paths are a further important element, for these allow you to enter and explore the miniature universe of the water garden, and they are designed as features in their own right, with elaborate patterns of pebbles, cobbles and even mosaics. The overall impact is one of balance, with just the right number of plants growing in a natural landscape that inspires calmness and contemplation.

A Japanese garden (illustrated)

The same sensitivity for natural surroundings and a desire to create a miniature replica of wild scenery, motivate Japanese gardens, although the rules of composition are more strict and elaborate. These rules have evolved around the religious ideal of paradise as a huge water garden, and many of the elements have profound symbolism. At its simplest, a Japanese garden can be created in a small space, using moving water to represent the active force *(yang)* and areas of still water for the contemplative side of life *(yin)*. Large weathered stones stand for large terrestrial features such as mountains, while sand, gravel and cobbles imitate the lower, softer land forms. The overall design is imaginative and irregular, representing an extensive landscape in miniature and punctuated by human symbols such as a stone lantern or small arching bridge, a bamboo deer scarer (see p82) or strategically placed ladle and stone wash basin *(tsukubai)*.

practical
project
1

DESIGNING AN
ORIENTAL POND
continued

ESSENTIAL ELEMENTS

■ **Water** Aim for simplicity and informality – you will usually have to use a flexible liner to create your own design. Edge still pools with flat stone slabs for access, and add rocks and stones to running water.

■ **Rocks** Try to choose rugged irregular samples for mountainous scenery and smooth well-worn examples for placing in or beside the water. Arrange some in a shallow stream bed to create noisy turbulence.

■ **Sand and gravel** Buy large-grained sand and gravel about 2.5cm (1in) in diameter for small open areas. Dot one or two mounds of soil and rocks within these to plant with moss or miniature trees.

■ **Stepping stones** Place these at convenient distances in stretches of turf or moss for dry-shod access. Broken stone slabs can be used to make crazy paving paths.

■ **Stone ornaments** Add authenticity with a few carefully placed ornaments such as a tower or well, together with the lantern and wash basin always found in Japanese tea gardens.

■ **Water features** Stepping stones in the water, timber decking at its edge and a bridge over a stream (see p106–7), together with waterfalls (see p140) are all extra elements that blend with the oriental style.

PLANTS FOR ORIENTAL GARDENS

Massed arrangements of varied water species are incompatible with oriental ponds, where a limited selection of plants is carefully positioned to enhance and complement a unified composition. Moss and close-cropped turf are used in open areas, often relieved by bonsai or solitary conifers, especially dwarf pines which represent silence and solitude. Bamboos, plums and cherries are authentic larger plants, azaleas are favourite flowering shrubs, and box hedging is often clipped strictly into rounded shapes. Most plants are grown on the banks, rather than in the water, and marginals are used sparingly: a group of irises, perhaps, and one or two ferns or ornamental grasses are sufficient.

The choice of specimen plants is limited and usually made from the following species: acer, astilbe, bamboos, camellia, fatsia, hibiscus, hosta, hydrangea, lilac, lilies, osmanthus, pieris, tree-peonies, primulas, prunus, rhododendrons, water lilies, willows.

MAKING A DEER SCARER

The traditional shishi odoshi, *or deer scarer, is a popular and effective device originally used by farmers to scare wild deer away from their crops. A length of thick bamboo, sealed at one end and hollowed out at the other (tapered) end, is set on a stand fitted with an axle so that the sealed end of the tube rests on a small stone. Water is led from a waterfall or overflow through a hollow bamboo pipe and drips into the tapered cavity, where it accumulates until its weight tips the tube to empty the water. As the empty tube springs back, its sealed end strikes the stone with a sharp crack – fix a metal stud in the end for a louder report.*

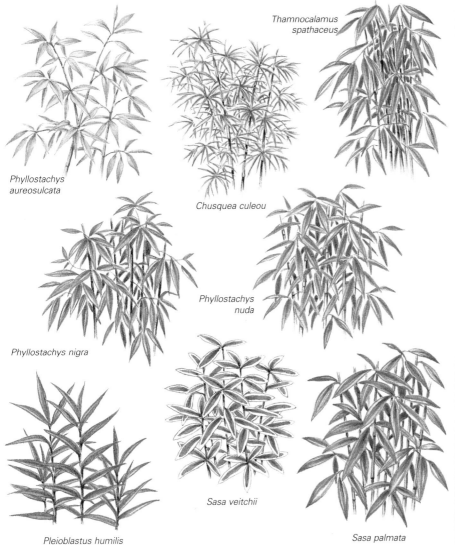

Phyllostachys aureosulcata

Thamnocalamus spathaceus

Chusquea culeou

Phyllostachys nuda

Phyllostachys nigra

Sasa veitchii

Pleioblastus humilis

Sasa palmata

BAMBOOS FOR ORIENTAL GARDENS

[Note: bamboo classification is very confused and the same plant is likely to be known by several different names]

Chusquea culeou – leafy olive-green branches
Phyllostachys aureosulcata – tall, golden stems
Phyllostachys nigra – graceful, mottled stems
Phyllostachys nuda – tall, powdered white stems
Pleioblastus humilis var. ***pumilus*** (syn. ***Arundinaria humilis***) – compact, clump-forming
Thamnocalamus spathaceus (syn. ***Fargesia murelliae***) – tall and arching
Sasa palmata – shining, purple-streaked stems
Sasa veitchii – dwarf, papery leaves

Bamboos

Bamboos are evergreen perennial grasses, authentic when planted in oriental gardens but equally suitable for any pond design. Most enjoy moist soils, but choose species with care because many are also very invasive and their creeping rhizomes may need trimming back annually with a spade. Some of the hardiest and best-behaved kinds are listed in the margin.

KOI CARP

Although the familiar goldfish is an acceptable choice for oriental water gardens, in larger ponds many enthusiasts prefer to keep brightly coloured Koi (or Nishikigoi) carp. These Japanese fish are often very large, up to 60–90cm (2–3ft) in length, and for good health need very extensive ponds with a minimum depth at the centre of 1.2–1.5m (4–5ft). However, two or three very young carp can be kept in a pond with a surface area of at least 4.5m^2 (50ft^2) until they are about 30cm (12in) long. They also need an efficient filtration system, because they tend to stir up any soil in the pond and produce large amounts of waste matter. Their diet is omnivorous and they will eat any plants growing in the pond, so keeping them is a specialist occupation.

plants
OF THE
month
2

PURPLE LOOSESTRIFE
(Lythrum salicaria)

Choice and prolific, often found in the wild but equally at home in garden surroundings. The simple species is a large and handsome plant, although compact cultivated forms are more suitable for smaller ponds.

type	Hardy herbaceous perennial; bog plant
flowers	Starry blooms, pinkish purple and long-lasting, on spikes up to 90cm (3ft) long; mid-summer to early autumn
foliage	Dark green, narrow and spear-shaped, on erect downy stalks in clumps
height	Up to 1.5m (5ft)
spread	75cm (30in)
position	Full sun or light shade, in fairly rich moist or wet soil (even tolerates temporary submersion), in larger bog gardens and at water's edge
planting	Autumn or spring, 60cm (2ft) apart, in small groups of one colour only for best effect
care	Mulch with compost in autumn and feed with a general fertilizer in spring. Cut back all growth to ground level in autumn. Pull up or transplant seedlings while young
propagation	Seeds (species only) sown in autumn in a cold frame; division in autumn or spring
related plants	Many shorter and more colourful garden forms, including 'Feuerkerze' ('Firecandle'), red; 'Lady Sackville', rose-pink; 'Robert', clear pink; 'The Beacon', crimson

LIZARD'S TAIL
(Saururus cernuus)

The shapely foliage looks fresh all season, but the main attraction is the summer crop of graceful and appealing flowers. Ideal for larger ponds, but may be invasive elsewhere.

type	Hardy herbaceous perennial; bog and marginal plant
flowers	Small, creamy white and fragrant, in fluffy spikes like thin tails; early to late summer
foliage	Rich olive-green, large and heart-shaped, turning crimson in autumn
height	60cm (2ft)
spread	30–60cm (12–24in), to 1.5m (5ft) if unrestricted

Lizard's tail

Chinese loosestrife

position	Full sun or moderate shade, in rich moist or wet soil, in larger bog gardens, and in shallow water, depth 0–10cm (0–4in)
planting	Spring, 45cm (18in) apart, in small groups direct into the soil where space is not limited, or in baskets
care	Feed in spring with a general fertilizer. Cut down all growth in autumn
propagation	Division in spring
related plants	*S. chinensis* is a similar Asian species

CHINESE LOOSESTRIFE
(Lysimachia clethroides)

Much less invasive than some of the loosestrifes, this is breathtaking in summer when covered in long spikes of white flowers, just like a dwarf buddleja.

type	Hardy herbaceous perennial; bog plant
flowers	White, tiny and star-shaped, on long arching spikes; mid-summer to early autumn

foliage	Bright green and lance-shaped, turning orange-red in autumn
height	60–75cm (24–30in)
spread	60cm (24in)
position	Full sun or shade, in most moist soils that are not too alkaline, under trees or beside the water's edge
planting	Autumn or spring, 30cm (12in) apart, in groups
care	Mulch in autumn and feed with a general fertilizer in spring
propagation	Division in autumn or spring
related plants	*L. punctata*, with upright growth and yellow flowers, and white *L. ephemerum* are less invasive than most other species

RAGGED ROBIN ▶
(Lychnis flos-cuculi)

A quietly attractive flower of marshes and damp places, not one of the more spectacular and yet always welcome and lovely in a wild waterside context.

type	Hardy herbaceous perennial; bog plant
flowers	Large, pink and fringed, on long reddish stalks; late spring to mid-summer
foliage	Narrow and sparse, in a thin clump
height	60cm (2ft)
spread	30cm (12in)
position	Full sun or light shade, in any moist or wet soil, best beside wildlife ponds
planting	Autumn or spring, 15cm (6in) apart, in small groups or patches, in any moist soil
care	Undemanding. Cut down all growth in autumn
propagation	Seeds sown in a cold frame in spring; division in autumn or spring
related plants	Dwarf 'Nana' and white-flowered *albiflora*; *L. × arkwrightii* and *L. × haageana* are both shorter, orange-flowered hybrids

GREATER SPEARWORT ▶
(Ranunculus lingua 'Grandiflorus'*)*

Most spearwort and buttercup species can be irrepressible invaders, but this one compensates for any colonial tendencies by having the showiest flowers of all.

type	Hardy herbaceous perennial; marginal and shallow aquatic

flowers	Large, 5cm (2in) across, bright yellow and shining, on branching stalks; mid-spring to early autumn
foliage	Long and tongue-shaped, bright green but pinkish in spring
height	60–90cm (2–3ft)
spread	30cm (12in)
position	Full sun or light shade, at the edge of larger ponds and in water, depth 5–30cm (2–12in)
planting	Spring, 23cm (9in) apart, in small groups, direct into the soil, or in baskets in smaller ponds
care	Cut back all growth in autumn. Divide vigorous clumps every 3–4 years
propagation	Seeds sown in a cold frame in spring; division in spring
related plants	*R. flammula* (Lesser Spearwort) is less vigorous but also less colourful; *R. aquatilis*, see p23

practical project 2

INSTALLING AND USING ELECTRICITY

It is not essential to have electricity laid on in the water garden, and perhaps the majority of ponds give enormous pleasure and satisfaction without further embellishment. But providing a source of power is the first priority if you decide to incorporate a moving water feature such as a fountain, waterfall or stream, or to install lighting.

A temporary extension lead may be adequate for occasional lighting or for running a pond heater – for safety always use a heavy-duty earthed cable plugged in via a residual current device (RCD) which will break the circuit in a few milliseconds in the event of mishap. Permanent features require a more elaborate arrangement of mains or low-voltage wiring installed to an acceptable standard. It is best to leave mains wiring to a qualified electrician, or at least have your own work inspected by a professional before use to avoid possibly fatal consequences (see margin). However, you can certainly fit a permanent low-voltage circuit yourself and also undertake some of the preparatory work for a mains system.

LOW-VOLTAGE CIRCUITS

Most garden lighting and some pumps operate on 12 or 24 volts, supplied from the mains and stepped down through a transformer. These are very safe systems that do not require armoured or protected cables, and you can install them yourself. Most transformers are intended for indoor use –

although some weatherproof models are available. They are simply plugged into a mains socket, preferably with an RCD for additional safety, and the low-voltage supply lead is ducted outdoors, ideally in plastic conduit to avoid accidental damage, and may then be buried in the soil or disguised by plants or stones until it reaches the pond. Always use waterproof connectors when joining cables and protect each joint from rainfall with a stone slab or slate.

MAINS-VOLTAGE CIRCUITS

An outdoor mains circuit should be laid underground, because overhead cables are both unsightly and unsafe. Fully armoured cable is housed in plastic conduit and buried in a trench at least 60cm (2ft) deep beneath lawns and cultivated soil, 45–50cm (18–20in) deep under hard surfaces such as paths. Buried sections are covered with a protective layer of roof tiles marked with brightly coloured warning tape before refilling the trench.

Indoors, connection is made to the mains consumer unit through a dedicated switching unit fitted with a fuse and RCD. At the other end, where the cable rises to the surface, a weatherproof socket can be fitted on a wall or post, or connection can be made direct to an above-ground pump chamber, although the latter arrangement often then precludes plugging in other equipment such as a pond heater.

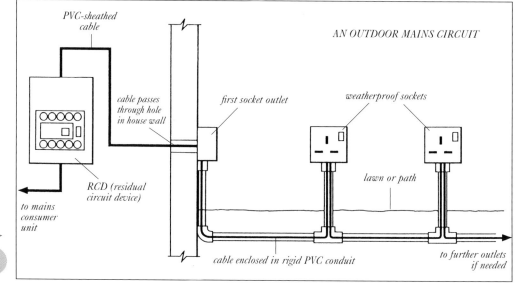

AN OUTDOOR MAINS CIRCUIT

PVC-sheathed cable

cable passes through hole in house wall

first socket outlet

weatherproof sockets

RCD (residual circuit device)

to mains consumer unit

lawn or path

cable enclosed in rigid PVC conduit

to further outlets if needed

PUMPS

Unless you have access to a natural source of flowing water, a pump is essential for circulating water to fountains, waterfalls and artificial streams. Most pumps work in the same way: water is drawn in through an input strainer by a rotary impeller driven by an electric motor, and forced out again under pressure through an outlet or delivery pipe. An adjustable tap for regulating the flow of water is usually an integral part of the unit and there are often separate outlets for a fountain or waterfall. Extra units can sometimes be powered by adding a T-shaped coupling to the delivery pipe.

There are two types of pump:
Submersible models must be operated under water and are usually silent and self-priming, as well as inexpensive and easy to install.

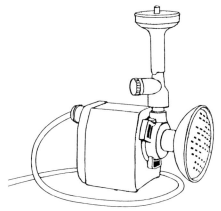

Submersible pump which has a fountain head fitted

Surface pumps are often more powerful and may be positioned above or below ground but always in a dry, ventilated chamber; if sited above water level, a footvalve must be fitted to maintain the prime (keep the pump filled with water).

BIOLOGICAL FILTERS

Keeping the water clean in fish ponds, especially those housing Koi carp, involves some kind of filtration. In small ponds, mechanical filters are efficient and inexpensive. Some are units within which water is drawn through charcoal or gravel, while others are made of plastic foam or a similar porous material attached to the strainer covering the water inlet on a pump. Whenever this is switched on, the filter passively sifts out particles of soil, waste material and algae, producing beneficial results fairly quickly.

Biological filters are more complex and depend on resident bacteria actively feeding on potentially toxic matter such as fish excreta, which is eventually transformed into harmless waste. The filtration unit can be sited outside the pond or submerged on the bottom, but in all cases a continuous flow of water through the unit must be supplied via a pump for the bacteria to thrive. There is often no noticeable impact until several weeks after installation.

HEATERS

Keeping the pond from freezing over completely in winter is a high priority if you keep fish; there are various ways of doing this (see p12). If you have a power supply laid on for a pump, installing an electric pool heater becomes an easy and reliable option. This will usually consist of a straight rod element fitted through a wooden or polystyrene float which keeps the heater at surface level. It is plugged in directly to the mains supply and left in position whenever hard frost is forecast.

SAFETY GUIDELINES

Water and electricity are a potentially lethal combination, so make sure you always follow these simple rules.

■ *Only use equipment and materials specifically designed for use outdoors*

■ *Make sure all equipment is made to the relevant safety standard and properly earthed*

■ *Follow directions for installation precisely*

■ *Fit a residual current device or circuit breaker with a trip rating of 30mA to protect yourself from shocks*

■ *Use heavy-duty or armoured cable for all outdoor supplies*

■ *All joints, couplings and switches must be waterproof*

■ *Keep and display a record of where cables are buried*

■ *Maintain equipment regularly and check for any damage before use*

LIGHTING EFFECTS
Outdoor lighting, installed under water or above ground, can produce spectacular effects in the water garden: for details, see p107.

AUGUST

There are few urgent maintenance tasks this month, allowing plenty of opportunities to relax and watch the progress of pond life. If you have a collection of fish of both sexes, they will certainly have spawned and produced tiny fry by now. Their lives at this stage are perilous, for they supply food for a wide variety of insects, larvae and even adult fish. Fortunately they are produced in such large numbers that many manage to survive and those that do will be the fittest, the ones that were most successful at escaping or camouflaging themselves in submerged plant growth.

Adult fish may come to the surface now to take gulps of fresh air; usually an indication of oxygen shortage in the water. Playing a jet from a hosepipe on the surface for a short while and making sure you have a full complement of oxygenating plants will relieve this seasonal deficiency. Running water is rarely short of oxygen, and adding features such as a fountain or waterfall can prevent lack of aeration as well as increasing your enjoyment of the pond. Moving water is soothing on the ear, offering pleasures that are quite different from those of still, serene pools; it also cools the air to bring some relief from the dry heat typical of many late summer days.

The water world constantly changes as the seasons progress, varying from inundation in winter, for example, to shrinking water levels and marginal drought at this time of year. Happily many of the pond organisms have adapted their lifecycles to intermittent desiccation, some of the smallest changing into drought-resistant forms that can remain dormant until they miraculously reappear when water levels rise again. For others maturity coincides with the dry season, and you will often see caddisfly nymphs climbing out on tall leaves for their final transformation before flying away, while the air above the pond will be alive with newly emerged mosquitoes and midges dancing in the evening warmth.

tasks

FOR THE

month

GOING ON HOLIDAY
Although life in the pond is very hectic at the moment, little will suffer if you are away for a week or two. Provided there are plenty of water plants of all kinds, fish can manage for a fortnight without supplementary feeding, but it is a good idea to ask a neighbour or friend to switch on any aeration device for a short while now and then, or simply to empty a canful of water into the pond should there be problems with de-oxygenation. Make sure any seedlings and young plants in the course of propagation are covered with enough water in their trays, and keep them out of the sun to reduce evaporation.

CHECKLIST

- [ ] Check and prune water lilies
- [ ] Take care of young fish
- [ ] Look in the mornings for signs of overnight fish problems
- [ ] Making an underwater viewer
- [ ] Consider the safety of children

WATER LILY CARE

By now, vigorous water lily growth has often caught up with flowering and the large lily pads may begin to obscure late summer buds and blooms. At the same time, leaves which developed earlier in the season are starting to fade and disintegrate with age. Try tidying up larger plants by removing any discoloured leaves and also some of those congesting the flowers, using a sharp knife tied to end of a long cane if you cannot reach the plants comfortably. This light pruning does not harm plants and will improve their appearance for the rest of the flowering season.

Watch out for any signs of leaves and flower stems turning black and starting to rot, especially on yellow-flowered varieties. This may be the first symptoms of water lily crown rot, a serious disease causing the whole rootstock to decay eventually into a foul-smelling mass of jelly. Plants affected by this must be destroyed by burning, the soil in which they grew should be dispersed elsewhere in the garden, and their containers should be sterilized with bleach or disinfectant before re-use. A more virulent (but less common) form of the disease affects all kinds of water lily equally, rapidly turning plants into a brown unpleasant mass.

LOOKING AFTER YOUNG FISH

Given a balanced population of sexually mature fish (those over about 8cm (3in) long), spawning can be expected to take place any time from mid-spring until this month, depending on water temperatures, daylight length and a number of other factors. By now small fry should be seen swimming or hiding in submerged plant growth.

At this stage they are very vulnerable and many fall prey to various predators, but their numbers are so large that enough usually survive to grow into adult fish — these are the ones that were most successful at hiding or eluding capture, or that were simply lucky. Dedicated enthusiasts take all kinds of precautions to ensure their survival, including hand-rearing them in separate tanks, but most water gardeners prefer not to interfere and leave them to

take their chance in the natural way.

The simplest method of encouraging fish to spawn and also to help the fry survive is to provide a shallow shelf area at one side of the pond and stock it well with marginal plants. The water here will become warmer and adult fish can use the area for courtship and for attaching their eggs to plants floating near or at the surface. Once hatched, the fry will spend a lot of time here in the safety of the plant growth.

They need no feeding at first while they are supported by the yolk sacs; special fry food is available to give to them over the next three weeks or so, although very often they will scavenge successfully for themselves. By the time they are about six weeks old, they can be considered relatively safe and self-sufficient.

OVERNIGHT FISH CASUALTIES

Submerged plants are essential for providing a continuous supply of the dissolved oxygen needed by fish and other pond fauna (see p77). But sometimes in warm weather dead fish may be found floating on the surface in the mornings, even though the pond is well stocked with healthy plants and the water quality is good. The largest fish usually succumb first, while smaller ones are found

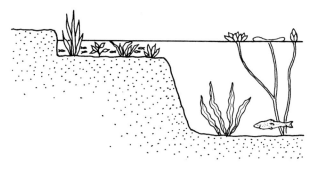

Provide a shallow shelf for small fry

gulping air at the surface or clustered round the outflow of a pond filter.

This often happens because submerged plants emit oxygen during daylight while photosynthesizing, but at night they produce carbon dioxide, the same gas as fish breathe out all the time. Under normal conditions the pond as a whole absorbs oxygen from the atmosphere and releases carbon dioxide, but this process can be obstructed in late summer by close thundery weather so carbon dioxide accumulates overnight. Fish and submerged plants add to this gas gradient leading to an excess of carbon dioxide in the water, with the result that larger fish (whose need for oxygen is greatest) are asphyxiated. A calm surface aggravates the problem, whereas any agitation helps release the gas, and the best remedy in still humid weather is to play water from a hose over the surface last thing at night and again early in the morning. Leaving a fountain or waterfall running gently at night will help, as will special airstones that can be bought for placing in the pond to break the surface.

AN UNDERWATER VIEWER

Much of the activity in a pond takes place underwater, often only just out of sight — since refraction of daylight at the surface distorts images, even nearby objects are often difficult to see clearly. An easy way to watch life in a pond is to use a small plastic aquarium, weighted with one or two heavy stones so that the bottom floats a little way below the surface and offers a window on the underwater scene. You can make your own with a large clear or translucent plastic drum: cut off the bottom and replace this with clear plastic secured in place with glue or waterproof

Looking through the viewer

tape. If pushed into the water and held a little way below the surface, this will reveal a surprising amount of normally unseen activity.

PONDS AND SMALL CHILDREN

Exploring water in any shape or form is an irresistible temptation, and considerations of safety must be paramount wherever small children come into contact with ponds, especially at this time of year when schools are on holiday. The only certain insurance is for an adult to be present when children are near the pond, but there are other important precautions that can help reduce the risks.

SAFETY MEASURES

■ Shelve the sides gently wherever the pond is easily accessible, so that the water is very shallow for a distance of at least 60cm (2ft) out from the bank — remember it is possible to drown in less than 15cm (6in) of water
■ Make sure banks, edging stones, perimeter paths and any kind of viewing platform or bridge are all kept sound and well maintained; all parts of electrical equipment must be safe, and preferably inaccessible or out of sight
■ Since very young children have little concept of danger, you might prefer to erect a barrier part or all of the way round the pond in the form of a fence, hedge or wall. This could be a temporary precaution, or with imagination a permanent feature blending with the layout. For older children, a psychological barrier such as a row of spaced, partly buried posts might be sufficient reminder of the proximity of water
■ Consider installing lighting to improve visibility after dark
■ Above all, teach children clearly and repeatedly about the risks, and the dangers of falling even into shallow water; devise a simple code of behaviour at the water's edge and firmly enforce it

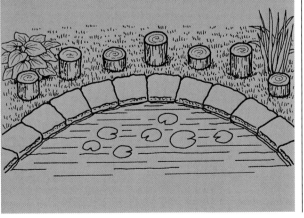

WATCH OUT FOR
The disorientated water hawthorn
The fragrant water hawthorn, Aponogeton distachyos (see p116), is a native of South Africa and has not acclimatized to more temperate flowering seasons. After the main spring crop of blooms, plants gently disintegrate until late summer, when they often disappear from sight altogether unless growing in shade. By mid-autumn however, they have usually produced a fresh set of leaves and start flowering again, sometimes through to early winter or later in mild gardens. Meanwhile floating fruits from the earlier flowers begin to disperse and may be netted for autumn sowing in pots.

plants

OF THE

month

1

Primula japonica

PRIMULAS

Most primulas enjoy rich moist soil, some the even dampness of deciduous woodlands and others the icy cold melt of alpine snowlines. But there is a large group that are definite bog garden species, thriving where the ground is cool and moisture-retentive, though not in the soggy wet soil of marginal sites. Some are elusive and temperamental, but here are a few of the more easily-grown and lovely species that are essential for the well-stocked bog garden. They all share common characteristics.

CULTIVATION
of Primulas

type	Hardy evergreen perennials; bog plants
foliage	Bright green and soft, long and oval, in rosettes that usually persist over winter
position	Full sun to moderate shade, in fairly rich soil with added compost, evenly damp and not too alkaline
planting	Autumn or spring, 15–23cm (6–9in) apart, in natural drifts and groups
care	Mulch with garden compost in spring, every other year alternating with a feed of general fertilizer. Leave flowerheads to set and disperse seeds before cutting down. Divide every 4–5 years
propagation	Seeds surface-sown in a cold frame when ripe or in early spring (see p40); division in autumn or spring

Primula aurantiaca

A candelabra with striking bright orange or orange-red blooms in tiers on tall stems, flowering slightly earlier than other similar kinds – late spring and early summer.

height	45–75cm (18–30in)
spread	30cm (12in)

Primula beesiana

A vigorous and freely self-seeding mid- to late summer candelabra with rich mauve or rosy purple flowers with a yellow eye, gathered in 6–8 whorls of small blooms.

height	60–75cm (24–30in)
spread	30cm (12in)
related plants	Crosses with orange *P. bulleyana* to produce the attractive hybrid *P.* × *bulleesiana* (below)

Primula × *bulleesiana*

A very easy bog primula for consistently damp soil, a natural hybrid producing a wide spectrum of coloured candelabras, from yellow and orange through to red and purple, in early and mid-summer.

height	60cm (2ft)
spread	30cm (12in)
related plants	The beautiful 'Asthore Hybrids' are perhaps the best selection

DRUMSTICK PRIMULA
(Primula denticulata)

The well-known Drumstick Primula, with neat spherical heads, 8cm (3in) across, of white, blue, red or lilac flowers on stout short stems, in spring just as snowdrops are finishing.

height	30cm (12in)
spread	30cm (12in)
related plants	Many garden forms, including 'Glenroy Crimson', 'Robinson's Red' and 'Snowball'

HIMALAYAN COWSLIP
(Primula florindae)

The superb Himalayan Cowslip, flowering early to late summer with slightly powdery, sulphur-yellow blooms in a single, sometimes two-tiered umbel, followed by handsome seedheads. Spectacular when grown en masse beside running water.

height	60–90cm (2–3ft)
spread	45cm (18in)
related plants	Various un-named hybrids, and red and orange selections are sometimes available

Primula japonica

Probably the best-known candelabra, with lush cabbage-like leaves and several whorls of red, pink or white blooms, opening in stages in early and mid-summer. Best in partial shade.

height	60–90cm (2–3ft)
spread	30–45cm (12–18in)
related	Many good selections, including

plants 'Alba', 'Apple Blossom', 'Miller's Crimson' and 'Postford White'

Primula pulverulenta

A tall species that flowers immediately after *P. japonica*, with several whorls of pink or mauve flowers with dark eyes, held on white powdery stems. Best in shade unless planted in very moist soil.

height	90cm (3ft)
spread	45cm (18in)
related plants	'Bartley Hybrids', mixed colours, and 'Bartley Pink', very pale pink with orange eyes

Primula rosea

Small and dainty like a primrose, for waterside rockeries and less congested areas of the bog garden. The low rosettes of foliage are smothered in early spring with bright rosy pink blooms that are yellow-eyed and conspicuous.

height	15cm (6in)
spread	15cm (6in)
related plants	'Grandiflora', which has larger flowers

Primula sikkimensis

A fragrant species from wet Far Eastern meadows, like a smaller version of the Himalayan Cowslip, with variable bright yellow flowers in late spring. A long-lived primula for waterside planting.

height	45cm (18in)
spread	30cm (12in)
related plants	Several slightly different selections, often identified by collectors' numbers, illustrate the variable size and colour of blooms

ORCHID PRIMULA
(Primula vialii)

Quite distinct from other species, the Orchid Primula has startling spikes of bright red buds, like a Red Hot Poker *(Kniphofia)*. These open from early summer onwards as mauve or lilac blooms, making an attractive contrast with the buds.

height	30–45cm (12–18in)
spread	30cm (12in)

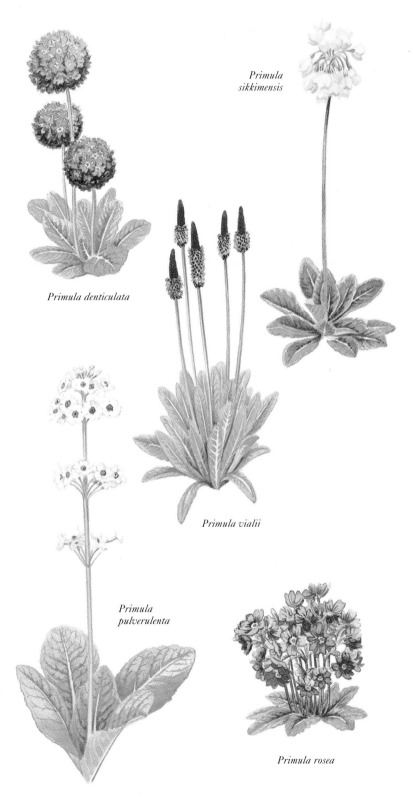

Primula sikkimensis

Primula denticulata

Primula vialii

Primula pulverulenta

Primula rosea

practical
project
1

MAKING A MINIATURE
WATER GARDEN

Cross-section through a tub garden

Cross-section through a tyre garden

Ponds do not have to be large and ambitious: mini ponds are feasible projects that provide enough room for several decorative plants or a few tiny goldfish, and with a little ingenuity one could be accommodated in the smallest garden, patio or even on a balcony. For practical purposes, containers should be totally waterproof and weather-resistant, and have a minimum capacity of about 27 litres (6 gallons). They may be purpose-built, using a flexible liner or preformed shell, or alternatively you could recycle a container such as a sink, half-barrel or old car tyre, as these projects suggest.

A POND IN A POT

Perhaps the smallest of feasible mini-ponds, this uses a 60cm (24in) clay pot, partly buried in the ground and fitted with a bubble fountain or a pump-driven water tap. Use an undrained pot or seal the drainage hole before sinking it in the ground, fit a pump of the appropriate size (see p86) and feed the cable inconspicuously over the side of the pot. Three-quarters fill with gravel, and on this space out small pots of dwarf grasses, sedges and trailing plants, before adding more gravel or pebbles to complete the arrangement. Some of the pebbles can be heaped in the centre around a bubble fountain jet, or a timber batten may be wedged at one side to support a tap fed from a length of pipe attached behind the batten.

A TUB GARDEN

Wooden tubs or half-barrels are traditionally used for water features in small gardens and on patios. Make sure yours has not been treated with preservative, and check that the wooden panels are tightly fitted and waterproof (test by filling with water and waiting for a few days for the wood to swell and seal any gaps); if leaks persist, line the container with plastic sheeting secured neatly just below the inside rim with thin laths or strips of hard plastic.

For durability the inside of new timber can be coated with bitumen paint, and the outside similarly, although this often looks more attractive if varnished. Old sherry and wine barrels should be in reasonable condition, their former contents acting as a preservative: for extra protection the inner surface can be charred with a blowtorch before filling with water.

There will be enough room in the tub for one or two dwarf water lilies, a couple of floaters and a clump of iris. As with all small containers, some form of winter insulation is essential if the tub is free-standing above ground.

A TYRE POND

Discarded car and lorry tyres make excellent and durable ponds. Several can be scattered throughout the garden, where they will be popular as bird baths as well as housing a number of smaller water plants. Excavate a hollow a little deeper than the tyre is wide, with a larger central cavity about 38–45cm (15–18in) deep, so that the tyre will sit on a shelf all round the perimeter. Line the hole with sand and a piece of strong plastic sheeting. Using a very sharp, strong knife remove the wire rim on one side by cutting through the tyre wall, then nestle the tyre, uncut side downwards, on the shelf; conceal the upper edge with large stones or slabs. Rocks and marginal plants grown in 15cm (6in) containers should tuck securely into the tyre at the edges, while a small deep water aquatic can sit in the centre, either in a basket or planted in a 5–8cm (2–3in) bottom layer of soil or aquatic compost.

A SINK GARDEN

An old glazed sink that is still waterproof is ideal as a raised pond when supported on bricks or sections of railway sleeper to keep the plughole off the ground – this can be blocked permanently or stopped with a plug for drainage and cleaning purposes. Scrub the sink inside and out, and rinse thoroughly. You can disguise the glazed outside with an artificial stone mixture, sometimes called hypertufa, made by mixing two parts peat with one part sand and one of cement (measured by volume while dry); mix with a little water to make a workable mortar. Coat the glazed surface with PVA glue and when this is tacky liberally trowel the hypertufa over the outer surfaces, over the top of the walls and 8–10cm (3–4in) down the inside, leaving the finish fairly rough. Allow several weeks for drying and then paint with a slurry of mud, yoghurt and cow manure to hasten a weathered appearance.

As there is no integral marginal shelf, plants can be stood in pots or small baskets on bricks to support them at their preferred depths.

A RAISED PATIO POND

A satisfying design compatible with a formal patio or terrace can be built in the same way as an indoor pond (see p132), using a rigid preformed shell or a flexible liner. The lower half of the pond sits in a shallow excavation made during construction of the patio, while the upper portion is housed in a simple enclosure of stone or brick. Cap the structure with suitable edging stones for a neat finish. Adaptations of this basic design can include adding a central, slightly concave stone to hold water pumped gently from below, or a short channel leading water to the pond from a higher pool or wall-mounted spout (see p124), the water in each case circulated by a pump concealed at the bottom of the main pond.

PLANTS FOR MINI-PONDS

Acorus calamus (p130)
Aponogeton distachyos (p116)
Butomus umbellatus (p78)
Calla palustris (p54)
Equisetum hyemale (p14)
Juncus effusus (p134)
Menyanthes trifoliata (p54)
Pistia stratiotes (p14)
Pontederia cordata (p79)
Typha minima (p139)
   many forms of pygmy water
   lilies (p71)

plants

OF THE

month

2

Siberian iris

SIBERIAN IRIS
(Iris sibirica)

Irises are essential waterside plants, and this is one of the easiest, less fussy than some about soil conditions and available in a huge range of gorgeous colours.

type	Hardy evergreen perennial; bog plant
flowers	Small, three-petalled and elaborately formed, violet-blue, cream or white in the plain species; late spring and early summer
foliage	Long and very narrow, in erect tufts
height	75cm (30in)
spread	30cm (12in)
position	Full sun or very light shade, in fairly rich damp soil, beside still or running water
planting	Early summer, 23cm (9in) apart, in groups, positioning the segments of rhizomes at the surface or no more than 5cm (2in) deep
care	Mulch with compost over winter in the first year, and thereafter in early summer after flowering. Cut down dead flowerheads and also any damaged leaves in late autumn. Divide and replant every 4–5 years
propagation	Division of rhizomes after flowering, replanting only young outer portions
related plants	There are many good hybrids, such as 'Perry's Blue', 'Purple Cloak', 'Southcombe White' and 'Sparkling Rosé'; *I. orientalis*, syn. *I. ochroleuca* (white and gold) enjoys very wet soil

WATER MINT
(Mentha aquatica)

This is so easy to grow that it can soon become invasive, and yet it is indispensable for covering the edges of ponds with its aromatic leaves and flowers that attract bees and other foragers.

type	Hardy herbaceous perennial; marginal and shallow aquatic
flowers	Tiny, pale mauve and fragrant, in tight rounded clusters arranged in whorls down the stalks; mid- and late summer
foliage	Dark green, small and oval, very aromatic when crushed, turning reddish purple in the sun
height	60–90cm (2–3ft)
spread	75cm (30in)
position	Full sun or semi-shade, in wet soil at the edge of larger ponds, or in water, depth 0–15cm (0–6in)
planting	Spring, in groups of three, direct into the soil beside large ponds, but safer in baskets to restrict growth
care	Cut down all growth in autumn. Divide every 3–4 years
propagation	Division or rooted stolons in spring
related plants	*M. pulegium* (Pennyroyal), dwarf and sprawling, also enjoys very moist soil

WATER PLANTAIN
(Alisma plantago-aquatica)

A lush and hardy plant for larger wildlife ponds, especially where volunteer plants are allowed to grow where they choose, for this species lavishly sets seeds that are dispersed by water.

type	Hardy herbaceous perennial; marginal and shallow aquatic
flowers	Three-petalled, 2.5cm (1in) across, white or pale pink, in large spreading panicles on 90cm (3ft) stalks; early summer to early autumn
foliage	Rich green, spear-shaped and ribbed, floating or on long stalks emerging from the surface
height	60–90cm (2–3ft)
spread	45cm (18in)
position	Full sun or semi-shade, in rich and very moist, slightly acid soil, or in water, depth 5–25cm (2–10in)
planting	Spring or early summer, 30cm (12in) apart, in groups, direct into the soil of large ponds, or in baskets
care	Deadhead immediately after flowering to prevent prolific self-seeding. Cut down all topgrowth in autumn
propagation	Seeds sown in a cold frame in autumn; self-set seedlings transplanted in early summer; division in spring
related plants	var. *parviflorum* has white or paler pink flowers on shorter stalks; *A. lanceolatum* is smaller with very slim leaves

BOG ASPHODEL
(Narthecium ossifragum)

A charming little wild flower of marshes and wet heaths, well suited to the damp margins of smaller ponds, especially when naturalized in drifts.

type	Hardy herbaceous perennial; bog and marginal plant
flowers	Small, star-shaped and six-petalled, orange or yellow in spikes on leafless stems; mid- and late summer
foliage	Narrow and sword-shaped, bright green with an orange tinge, in flattened tufts
height	15–23cm (6–9in)
spread	15cm (6in)
position	Full sun, in any wet soil, in bog gardens and near the edge of ponds, and also in water no deeper than 2.5cm (1in)
planting	Mid-spring, 10–15cm (4–6in) apart, in generous groups or drifts
care	Undemanding. Divide overcrowded clumps every 4–5 years
propagation	Seeds sown in very wet compost in a cold frame in spring; division in spring

(below left to right) Bog asphodel, water mint and water plantain

practical project 2

ATTRACTING
WILDLIFE
TO THE POND

Dragonflies – everyone's favourite, beautiful creatures with spectacular colours and larvae that live in underwater burrows waiting for small creatures to pass by; damselflies are closely related

You might be surprised to discover how quickly water insects, animals and even plants arrive to colonize a new pond. Flying insects such as beetles regularly take to the wing on warm days, frogs and newts are often found in moist areas of gardens a long way from any water, and dragonflies soon turn up if they are already breeding less than about three miles away. Plant seeds are carried on the wind or arrive as passengers on birds' feet, and even minute single-cell creatures dry up like dust and are blown from one pool to the next.

With this great diversity of life just waiting for a new habitat, deliberately setting out to attract wildlife might be thought unnecessary. Despite the growing interest in water gardening, however, many ponds are formal or inhospitable to all but the commonest wild species. Ideal water habitats are endangered ecosystems, many of them drying as the demand for ground water alters natural levels, while others are casualties of changing agricultural practices. Making a garden pond more inviting is a positive contribution towards countering this threat, and there are several things you can do without turning the garden into a wilderness.

THE LAND AROUND THE POND

As explained on pp56–7, a wildlife pond can be an attractive feature that harmonizes with many styles of garden, and the design criteria are undemanding. A natural pond by itself will invite many species to come and stay, but beyond the water's edge are other potentially attractive habitats for wildlife and small alterations to the fringe vegetation can yield rich dividends.

■ Whereas trees and their falling leaves can be a problem near formal ponds, they are an important part of wetland vegetation, providing shelter and forage for many insect species. Allow trees closest to the pond to cast a little shade, but prune or coppice any whose overhanging branches encourage stagnant areas. Where possible concentrate on introducing native species; avoid those with leaves likely to be poisonous to pond inhabitants including holly, horse chestnut, laburnum and rhododendron.

■ Rather than isolate the pond in neatly manicured surroundings, provide a buffer zone of semi-natural vegetation such as native shrubs, taller grass cut only once or

twice a year (a path kept mown short will provide access through the area), and wildflowers sown as a meadow or in large beds.

■ Create a bog garden at one end (see p68). This will soon develop into a lush area which, together with the tall grass and wildflowers, will act as a habitat for more secretive creatures. Frogs and toads, for example, will find shelter, winter quarters and a rich diet of insects. Don't forget some amphibians also enjoy warm sunny areas in summer, so include a stone or sand bank for them.

■ Although despised by tidy-minded gardeners, dead and decaying wood is a normal part of natural cycles, and can support many interesting fungi, mosses and insect all aiding its decomposition.

■ Avoid excessive tidiness in dedicated wildlife areas of the garden. Shade, litter and decay are key components of the natural world, and cutting down every dead stem in winter, for example, not only reduces frost protection for dormant perennials but also deprives hibernating insects of shelter. Aim for a balanced and acceptable level of planned neglect.

■ Introduce plants, both within the pond area and beyond, that will attract birds, butterflies and other creatures: shrubs with berries to feed birds in winter, or flat-headed flowers rich in nectar for browsing moths and hover-flies. The more species you can attract, the more inviting the water garden as a whole will appear to other wildlife.

FRIEND OR FOE?

If you want to help creatures settle in the water garden, you must suspend judgement over whether they are harmless allies or threatening pests. The distinction is hardly a valuable one anyway: as in the rest of the garden, everyone benefits from a stable food chain of prey and predator. Destroying all the aphids leaves blue tits and ladybirds without their favourite food, while a garden without slugs is unlikely to have resident frogs and toads, so do not try too hard to tame nature. Some pests can get out of hand, of course, but low population levels of most kinds are tolerable and encourage some of the following allies, many of which can be introduced in a bucket or two of water and mud from an existing wildlife pond.

WILDLIFE ALLIES

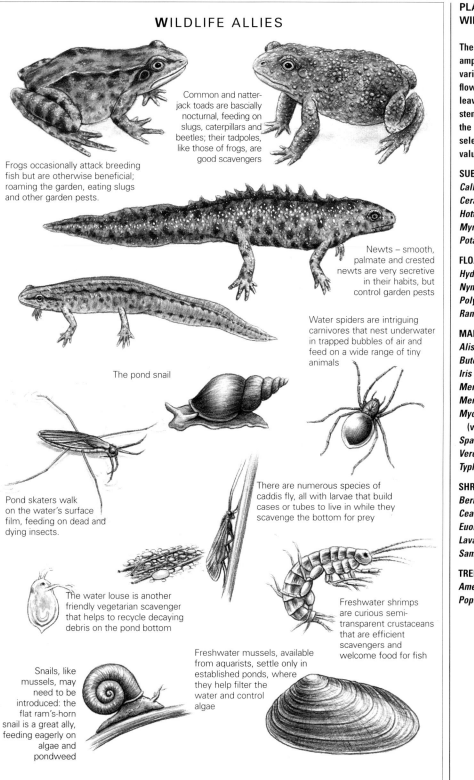

Frogs occasionally attack breeding fish but are otherwise beneficial; roaming the garden, eating slugs and other garden pests.

Common and natterjack toads are bascially nocturnal, feeding on slugs, caterpillars and beetles; their tadpoles, like those of frogs, are good scavengers

Newts – smooth, palmate and crested newts are very secretive in their habits, but control garden pests

The pond snail

Water spiders are intriguing carnivores that nest underwater in trapped bubbles of air and feed on a wide range of tiny animals

Pond skaters walk on the water's surface film, feeding on dead and dying insects.

There are numerous species of caddis fly, all with larvae that build cases or tubes to live in while they scavenge the bottom for prey

The water louse is another friendly vegetarian scavenger that helps to recycle decaying debris on the pond bottom

Freshwater shrimps are curious semi-transparent crustaceans that are efficient scavengers and welcome food for fish

Snails, like mussels, may need to be introduced: the flat ram's-horn snail is a great ally, feeding eagerly on algae and pondweed

Freshwater mussels, available from aquarists, settle only in established ponds, where they help filter the water and control algae

PLANTS TO ATTRACT WILDLIFE

The habits of pond insects and amphibians are widely varied; various species might need flowers for feeding, large floating leaves for shade or basking, or tall stems on which to emerge from the water. The following is just a selection of plants that are valuable in one way or another:

SUBMERGED PLANTS
Callitriche (water starwort)
Ceratophyllum (hornwort)
Hottonia (water violet)
Myriophyllum (water milfoil)
Potamogeton (pondweed)

FLOATING PLANTS
Hydrocharis (frogbit)
Nymphoides (fringed water lily)
Polygonum (bistort)
Ranunculus (water crowfoot)

MARGINALS
Alisma (water plantain)
Butomus (flowering rush)
Iris pseudacorus (yellow iris)
Mentha aquatica (water mint)
Menyanthes (bog bean)
Myosotis scorpioides
  (water forget-me-not)
Sparganium (bur-reed)
Veronica (brooklime)
Typha minima (lesser reedmace)

SHRUBS
Berberis; Buddleia; Caryopteris; Ceanothus; Cornus; Cotoneaster; Euonymus; Hebe; Hyssopus; Lavandula; Pyracantha; Sambucus; Spiraea; Viburnum

TREES
Amelanchier; Betula; Malus; Populus; Prunus; Salix; Sorbus

SEPTEMBER

Despite the occasional morning mist and hint of seasonal chill,
evenings this early in autumn are still warm enough for pond-
watching to be a pleasure. Ripeness is all and can be seen everywhere,
from the maturing fruits and seedheads on waterside plants to the
adult insects foraging among the leaves or dancing above the pond
surface in shafts of dying sunlight.

Light takes on a special quality at this time of year, with the sun's path
gradually dipping towards the horizon and the days gently shortening.
Colours become more intense in the golden light of autumn afternoons
and the brilliant turquoise, orange and crimson of blazing sunsets –
these are all reflected in the surface of a placid pool, creating graphic
sequences of moody colours and patterns inconceivable in the full glare
of summer.

Inspired designers, such as Japanese and medieval Moorish gardeners,
have played deftly with water to trap this natural drama, filling
shallow formal ponds to the brim and framing them with crisp edgings
to offer the largest mirror to the changing sky, so painting on the
surface a whole scene that is there one moment and then, at a touch or
a gentle breeze, suddenly shatters into a kaleidoscope of brilliant
fragments.

You can enhance this magical effect for autumn evenings by installing
subtle ambient lighting to illuminate the pool surface and adjacent
plantings, and to delay the moment when you have to go inside. This is
the hour when white flowers have their greatest impact, sparkling in
the twilight with an almost luminous intensity.

There is an increasing number of essential tasks to do from now on,
but they should not distract you just yet from the special moods and
colours of the pond in early autumn.

tasks
FOR THE
month

WATCH OUT FOR
Grazing caddisfly larvae
The larvae of various types of caddisfly construct 'cases' in which they live and feed on the pond bottom. In running water, a typical case is built with stones and sand grains, cemented with silk threads produced in the larva's mouth; the weight of these helps resist the tug of the water. In ponds the cases can be lighter and are often made of leaves. Watch carefully on a warm evening and you might see the creatures grazing on the algae on submerged stems and leaves: bubbles of air from the plants lodge in the case, helping the larva float up to new feeding grounds, until it reaches the surface where it ejects the bubbles and sinks to the bottom again.

CHECKLIST

- ☐ Clear decaying leaves and other vegetation
- ☐ Protect the pond against falling tree leaves
- ☐ Feed fish carefully to build up their strength
- ☐ Collect winter buds for propagation
- ☐ Examine dead frogs for signs of disease

START TIDYING UP FADING TOPGROWTH

Although many plants are still flowering in good condition, others will have started to fade and discolour as the nights cool and the days shorten. Opinions differ about whether to cut down the dead topgrowth of plants in autumn to keep the garden tidy, or to leave it until spring so that dormant crowns and roots receive some protection against frost.

Certainly, if the pond contains fish, it is important to prevent large amounts of the marginal dead leaves and blooms from falling into the water and accumulating as plant debris on the bottom: if the pond freezes above a lot of decomposing vegetation, the water quality can deteriorate alarmingly as potentially toxic gases build up under the ice, and fish will inevitably suffer.

Start, therefore, to cut and clear away any collapsing foliage and stems before they can enter the water; trim back fading marginal aquatics by two-thirds, but never cut them too low in case their hollow stems rot from being totally submerged. Leave one or two areas as cover for the various water animals that like to spend the winter in hiding near the banks — pests such as the water lily beetle will also overwinter there, but on balance these refuges shelter more allies than enemies.

NET AGAINST FALLING LEAVES

A few leaves in the water will add valuable new material to the bottom layer of silt in which so many plants and animals pass the winter, and will help sustain the natural food chains, but too much can be as detrimental as vegetation from marginal plants. The main fall of leaves from deciduous trees will not take place for a few weeks yet, but it is a good idea to take precautions now to prevent early heavy falls from sinking to the bottom out of reach.

Small mesh plastic or wire netting stretched across the pond is an effective barrier, especially if accumulations are raked off regularly to avoid shading the pond surface. The netting can remain in place all winter, if you choose, or it can be removed once the main fall of leaves is over. Waterside rock gardens should also be netted, since layers of wet leaves are lethal to many small alpines and rockery plants. Don't be too conscientious though — allow

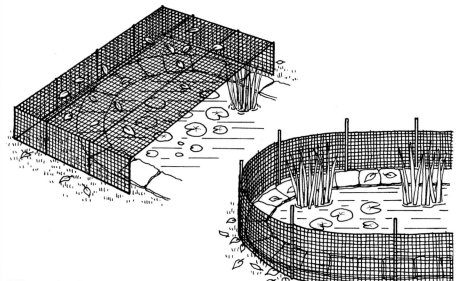

Different options for netting against falling leaves

some brightly coloured leaves from trees such as acers to reach the water surface as they add a beguiling, almost oriental charm to the overall appearance of the pond in autumn.

FEEDING FISH FOR STRENGTH

Well before water temperatures start to fall and induce winter inactivity in fish, you should take steps to build up their strength and food reserves while they still have good appetites. Continue giving them their normal ration of pellets or flakes every other day (see p41), but supplement this with high-protein foods that help increase their resistance to disease: dried ants' eggs, live *Daphnia*, shredded shrimps and worms are all suitable additions. It is still important to make sure no food is left in the water after about 20 minutes or so, and if the weather turns cold towards the end of the month, causing the fish to become less active, you should reduce the supplementary feeding accordingly for a while.

GATHERING DORMANT BUDS

Many floating and submerged aquatics produce offsets in the form of winter buds, variously known as 'turions' or 'bulbils' according to their structure — *Hydrocharis* (frogbit) and *Utricularia* (bladderwort) are typical of this type of plant. As autumn progresses, their winter buds sink to the bottom of the pond where they lie dormant until spring, so it is as well to start looking for them now if you want to propagate more plants by this method. Pick them off as you find them and overwinter them indoors. You can store them in a small jar of water in a cool frost-free place until the spring;

alternatively, spread them out on a thin bed of soil in a container of water in slightly warmer surroundings, where they will start into growth in late winter and make vigorous young plants for returning to the pond early next season.

LETHAL DISEASE OF FROGS

Frogs suffer from many problems apart from widespread loss of habitats,

which is unfortunate considering the benefits they bring to gardeners: any form of integrated management favours frogs and toads as a form of pest control. In recent years large numbers have died from a mysterious ailment, popularly known as 'red leg' because one of the symptoms is pronounced reddening of their thighs. This is thought to be caused by a bacterium which thrives in water low in oxygen or contaminated by heavy organic deposits. There is as yet no effective treatment, and in some seasons mass mortalities have caused considerable alarm among naturalists. Precautions gardeners can take include not transferring frogs or frog-spawn from one area to another, maintaining a healthy pond environment, and making sure that organic debris from dying plants and falling leaves does not build up at this time of year on the bottom of the pond.

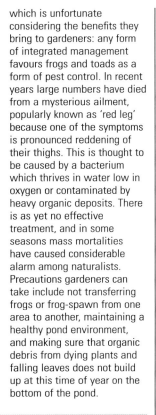

EMPTYING PONDS IN AN EMERGENCY

If a small pond has sprung a leak or the water quality is deteriorating because of a build up of silt, there is still time to clear it out while plants and fish remain active. The following steps should help to make a potentially complex and messy job very simple.

■ *Construct one or two temporary holding areas from plastic sheeting, large bowls or children's paddling pools*

■ *Remove marginal plants and deep water aquatics, dividing them if necessary, and keep in one of the pools*

■ *Floating plants and oxygenators can be collected and stored in containers of water*

■ *Start pumping or baling out the water until any fish can be seen and netted: keep these in a separate pool protected from predators. Save one or two bucketsful of pond water to add when refilling*

■ *Empty the pond and clear out the bottom mud. Wash down the liner and make any necessary repairs*

■ *Fill the pond once more, adding the samples of original pond water, and replant*

■ *Finally, add pool conditioner and wait the recommended length of time before reintroducing fish*

OTHER AUTUMN TASKS

After two or three months when the pond has sustained itself without much intervention, the number of tasks that need doing is beginning to increase. The following are some of those that might need attention soon, depending on the type of pond.

■ **In a warm season, pond levels could still need topping up occasionally**

■ **If the water temperature falls below 15°C (59°F) tropical fish should be returned to their winter quarters indoors**

■ **Continue removing blanketweed and other algae, and thin floating plants to reduce water surface cover**

■ **Detach young portions of tender aquatics such as *Pistia* and *Eichornia* for overwintering safely indoors**

■ **New ponds and water features may be constructed in spring or autumn, and now is a good time to start preparations**

■ **Divide overgrown marginal plants before the soil and water are too cold for replanting**

plants

OF THE

month

1

CARDINAL FLOWER
(Lobelia cardinalis)

The various aquatic lobelias are all stately gems with varying degrees of hardiness, with tall spires of bright eye-catching flowers in late summer. Gardeners often try to grow them in ordinary garden soil, but they are only really happy with their toes in the water.

type	Hardy or half-hardy herbaceous perennial; bog and marginal plant
flowers	Bright rich red and asymmetrical (like a salvia), clustered on tall spikes, in late summer and early autumn
foliage	Shining bronze- or reddish green, narrow and pointed
height	90cm (3ft)
spread	30cm (12in)
position	Full sun or very light shade, in rich moist soil in the bog garden, or at the edge of ponds in shallow water, depth 5–15cm (2–6in)
planting	Spring, 25cm (10in) apart, in bold groups, direct in the soil; in cold gardens plant in baskets that can be taken indoors in winter
care	Cut down all topgrowth in autumn and either mulch crowns with compost over winter, or keep baskets under glass in larger containers. Protect against slug damage
propagation	Seeds sown under glass in spring; soft cuttings under glass in summer; division in spring
related plants	*L. fulgens* is larger and more graceful, but less hardy; *L. siphilitica* is very hardy with violet-blue flowers. There are also many good hybrids such as 'Dark Crusader' (deep red), 'Queen Victoria' (tall, scarlet), 'Russian Princess' (pink), and the varied 'Compliment' series, easily raised from seed

JAPANESE WATER IRIS
(Iris laevigata)

This species represents those irises that like to grow in shallow water (for bog garden species, see p94), and is perhaps the loveliest, with many cultivated forms, some of them flowering twice in the same season.

type	Hardy semi-evergreen perennial; marginal and shallow water aquatic
flowers	Three-petalled complex blooms, clear blue with a yellow central

Japanese water iris

	line down each petal, and up to 12cm (5in) across on tall stems; mid-summer and sometimes again in early autumn
foliage	Long, narrow and sword-shaped, sheathed together at the base
height	Up to 60cm (2ft)
spread	25cm (10in)
position	Full sun or very light shade, in very wet soil beside all sizes of pond, or in water, depth 0–10cm (0–4in)
planting	Spring or immediately after flowering, with the rhizomes at or just below the surface, direct into the soil of larger ponds, or in baskets
care	Deadhead after flowering, and remove any discoloured leaves in autumn. Divide every 4–5 years
propagation	Division after flowering
related plants	Numerous varieties in white and shades of blue or reddish purple. Other good water irises include *I. pseudacorus* (Yellow Flag), very robust and yellow-flowered, and *I. versicolor* (American Blue Flag), more restrained, with red- or blue-flowered varieties

WATER FRINGE, FRINGED WATER LILY
(Nymphoides peltata)

A wonderful vigorous plant for covering the surface of new ponds, providing shade before true water lilies have established, but best grown in containers as the long creeping rhizomes can soon build large colonies.

type	Hardy herbaceous perennial; deep water aquatic

flowers | Bright golden yellow, 5cm (2in) across and about 10cm (4in) above the water, rather like a buttercup with fringed petals; mid-summer to mid-autumn

foliage | Small, floating, heart-shaped leaves, up to 10cm (4in) across, light green becoming darker with purple undersides

height | 10cm (4in)

spread | 60cm (2ft)

position | Full sun or light shade, in water depth 15–60cm (6–24in)

planting | Spring, as dormant rhizomes or young plants, in baskets

care | Remove dead foliage in autumn before it sinks. Lift and divide every 3–4 years

propagation | Division in late spring

related plants | 'Bennettii' is similar with larger flowers

PLANTAIN LILY
(*Hosta fortunei*)

All Hosta species and varieties are excellent foliage plants, providing good ground cover at the edge of ponds. They may take 2–3 years to get established and are always vulnerable to slugs, but their dramatic impact ensures their lasting popularity.

type | Hardy semi-evergreen perennial; bog plant

flowers | Delicately perfumed pendent bell-shaped flowers, mauve or white, in strong spikes; mid-summer to early autumn

foliage | Large, oval and pointed, with prominent ribs, ranging from plain bluish green to variegated yellow, cream or white

height | 45cm (18in) or more

spread | 45cm (18in)

position | Shade or semi-shade (full sun if kept very moist), in rich soil in bog gardens, as ground cover or in generous specimen groups

planting | Spring, 38cm (15in) apart, in groups, in well-dug moist soil fortified with plenty of humus

care | Mulch in spring with garden compost. Remove faded flower stems and also any discoloured leaves in autumn.

propagation | Division in spring

related plants | All varieties are attractive. Other fine species include *H. decorata*, leaves ribbed and cream-edged; *H. lancifolia*, narrow leaves; *H. sieboldiana*, large blue-green leaves and fine flowers; *H. undulata*, white-splashed leaves; and *H. ventricosa*, dark green with conspicuous flowers

practical project 1

ADDING SPECIAL
WATER GARDEN
FEATURES

Such is the compulsive appeal of water gardening that once the basic layout is complete, further improvements always suggest themselves, and there are many features that may be added to increase your enjoyment.

BUILDING TIMBER DECKING

Timber decking combines the natural beauty of wood with a means of providing a sympathetic waterside pathway or sitting area; it can also be used to hide pond edges and even build an attractive bridge for informal settings. It is made up from panels, whose construction is very simple.

■ Two sizes of sawn and treated timber are used: 100mm x 50mm (4in x 2in) for the joists, and 38mm x 19mm (1¹/₂in x ³/₄in) for the decking battens.
   Limit the length of each decking panel to about 2m (6¹/₂ft) and its width to 1m (39in).

■ Evenly space three joists for each panel, and use 5cm (2in) galvanised wire nails to pin the battens across the joists, 12mm (¹/₂in)

apart and slightly overhanging the outer joist on each side.
■ If the ends of the joists are exposed on any panels after the decking is assembled, cover them neatly with a scrap piece of wood.

■ Stain and seal the completed panels with several coats of preservative.

■ Position the finished panels on level ground, buried railway sleepers or, where used as a bridge, on a solid concrete foundation at each end. If panels overhang the water, support them on square timber legs planted in concrete blocks.

A SIMPLE BRIDGE

Kits are available for constructing small rustic or oriental-style bridges over a stream, but these often look out of proportion in smaller gardens, where a simpler bridge may be more in keeping while still adding charm to the water garden.
   In a rocky setting, a stone slab securely mortared at each end will blend well. A

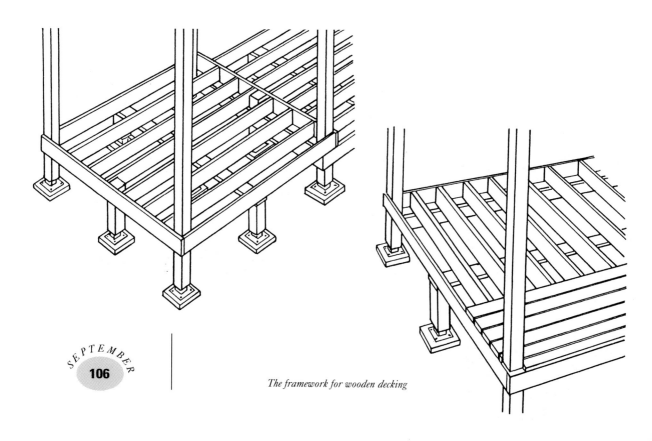

The framework for wooden decking

en footbridge can be made from railway sleepers or old floor joists laid parallel with their ends bedded in the ground in concrete – treat the timber with a suitable preservative. Thinner boards about 5cm (2in) thick may be nailed across two bearers made from 10–15cm (4–6in) diameter stakes for a similar effect.

For a more elaborate structure, fix strong crosspieces between square timbers set upright in concrete blocks, and cover with timber decking. In all cases safety is paramount and you should consider adding strong handrails.

ADDING STEPPING STONES

A series of stepping stones offers a magical way of crossing water, producing the illusion of a larger expanse of water and allowing you closer contact with the pond and its plants; in moving water they also create fascinating eddies and swirls. They are simple to install, provided you remember some simple guidelines.

■ They should be planned at an early stage because the water on all sides of the stones must be fairly shallow for safety (young children will be attracted by the adventure of crossing).

■ Each stone must be large enough to ensure a secure footing – about 38cm (15in) across is a minimum width; position one or two bigger ones where you are likely to stop and appreciate the scene. They must also be perfectly stable: make sure that the bottom of the pond is level, and bed them on two thicknesses of pond underlay to protect plastic liners.

■ Limit the distance between their centres to about 50cm (20in), which represents a comfortable stride.

■ Stones may be set at slightly different heights for variety, but no less than 5cm (2in) above the surface of the water.

■ Various materials are suitable – reconstituted stone, concrete, stone slabs on brick pillars, rounds of hardwood such as oak (char with a blowtorch and paint with bituminous compound for a long life).

■ Make sure the surface is rough for a good footing; timber sections should be covered with pieces of wire netting to prevent slipperiness.

LEVEL REGULATION AND OVERFLOWS

Although a pond can be filled or topped up with a hosepipe, and allowed to overflow into a bog garden when swollen after rain, adding an automatic level regulating system can save a lot of time and effort.

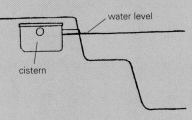

water level

cistern

For topping up you will need a cistern fitted with a ballcock. This is coupled to the mains water supply and positioned so that its outlet is at the pond surface level. When this level falls, the contents of the cistern begin to empty, causing the ballcock to fall and open the mains inlet valve.

For automatic drainage, feed a second pipe to the pond above the topping up pipe, and lead this to a soakaway or drain; cover the pond end with fine mesh as a filter.

For concrete ponds both pipes need to be in position during construction. Holes can be made in rigid and flexible liners for the pipes, which are fitted with special watertight washers which are self-sealing.

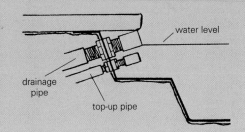

water level

drainage pipe

top-up pipe

LIGHTING THE WATER GARDEN

The possibilities for lighting the water garden are infinite, and the enormous range of spotlights, underwater floodlights, and even units for illuminating fountains with a sequence of changing colours, should meet every need. Some are equipped with spikes and are simply plunged into the soil, while others float on the water or can be weighted in position just below the surface for a more mysterious effect.

The secret of successful lighting is not to floodlight the whole garden, but just to pick out certain highlights and leave the rest in darkness for contrast. Remember that a spotlight produces a narrow, precisely focused beam, whereas floodlighting is diffused over a wide area. Low-voltage circuits are adequate for subtle or subdued lighting, typically using 25 watt bulbs on a 12V system, whereas more powerful units with 75–150 watt bulbs need mains electricity. The use of colour requires care – clear or white bulbs are usually preferable, although blue is dramatic and brighter shades can turn a fountain into a sensational feature.

plants

OF THE

month

2

LAVENDER MUSK
(Mimulus ringens)

All the numerous forms of mimulus like damp or wet conditions, but this is a true aquatic species, taller than most other kinds with more subtly coloured flowers.

type	Hardy herbaceous perennial; shallow water aquatic
flowers	Two-lipped like antirrhinums, lavender-blue, on slender erect branched stems; early summer to early autumn
foliage	Mid-green, oval or narrow, pointed and toothed, with prominent veins
height	60–90cm (2–3ft)
spread	60cm (2ft)
position	Full sun or moderate shade, at the edge of medium-sized or larger ponds, in patches in shallow water, depth 5–15cm (2–6in)
planting	Spring, 45cm (18in) apart, in small groups, direct in the soil or in baskets
care	Cut back all topgrowth in autumn. Divide every 3–4 years
propagation	Seeds sown in spring in a cold frame; soft cuttings under glass in summer; division in spring
related plants	Dwarf *M. luteus*, yellow with red blotches, is a good marginal plant; red *M. cardinalis* and *M. × bartonianus*, and rose-pink *M. lewisii* prefer bog garden conditions

HEMP AGRIMONY
(Eupatorium cannabinum)

A tall robust plant, too large for smaller ponds, but ideal in larger bog gardens or in the soil or shallow margins of larger wildlife ponds, where the pretty flowers attract butterflies.

type	Hardy herbaceous perennial; bog and marginal plant
flowers	Small, pink or red, in downy clusters at the top of tall branching stems; late summer to mid-autumn
foliage	Bright green and spear-shaped, serrated, on reddish erect stems
height	Up to 1.5m (5ft)
spread	60cm (2ft)
position	Full sun or light shade, in most kinds of damp soil, and in shallow water, depth 0–10cm (0–4in)
planting	Spring, 45cm (18in) apart, in groups of 2–3 plants
care	Mulch in autumn, and feed with a general fertilizer in spring. Deadhead to prevent prolific seeding, and cut down all growth in late autumn
propagation	Seeds sown in autumn or spring in a cold frame; self-set seedlings transplanted in spring; division in spring
related plants	'Album' is white and 'Flore Pleno' double-flowered. *E. purpureum* (Joe Pye Weed) is taller with rosy purple flowers, deep purple in subspecies *maculatum*; the form 'Atropurpureum' has purple leaves

MARSH ST JOHN'S WORT
(Hypericum elodioides, syn. *H. elodes)*

Most hypericums are showy perennial shrubs, but this aquatic relative is a diminutive creeper that is happy in mud or shallow water, and ideal for carpeting the edges of liners and filling in between larger strategic plants.

type	Hardy herbaceous perennial; bog and marginal plant
flowers	Small yellow trumpets at the tips of stems; mid-summer to early autumn
foliage	Small, oval and woolly, pale or greyish-green, in pairs on creeping stems
height	20–30cm (8–12in)
spread	45cm (18in)
position	Full sun or light shade, in any moist or wet soil, best en masse as a cover plant for pond edges or in water, depth 0–8cm (0–3in)
planting	Autumn or spring, 23cm (9in) apart, in groups, direct into the soil, or in baskets in small ponds
care	Undemanding. Tidy plants in autumn and divide every 4–5 years
propagation	Soft cuttings rooted in mud in summer; division in spring; rooted layers removed at any time
related plants	None which are suitable for water gardens

LIGULARIA, GOLDEN RAYS
(Ligularia dentata)

The large dramatic leaves of this well-built plant cover the surrounding soil and effectively suppress all weeds. In rich moist soil the plants make magnificent clumps that complement the stunning flowers late in the season.

type	Hardy herbaceous perennial; bog plant
flowers	Yellow and daisy-like, in large spreading heads on tall stems; mid-summer to mid-autumn
foliage	Large and rounded or heart-shaped, slightly cupped on strong stems, in handsome spreading clumps
height	90cm–1.2m (3–4ft)
spread	90cm (3ft)
position	Light or moderate shade with shelter from strong winds, in rich moist soil, in groups as ground

	cover or as specimen plants in bog gardens
planting	Autumn or spring, 75cm (30in) apart, in soil that has been well fortified with garden compost, decayed manure or leafmould
care	Mulch heavily in autumn with compost or decayed manure, and feed in spring with a general fertilizer. Cut back stems after flowering and clear all growth in late autumn. Divide clumps every 3–4 years
propagation	Seeds sown in a cold frame in spring; division in spring
related plants	The leaves of 'Desdemona' and 'Othello' are respectively purple and red beneath; *L. japonica* has large golden yellow starry flowers, *L. przewalskii* lemon-yellow spikes on black stems, and *L. veitchiana* round purplish leaves and yellow flowers in spikes

practical project 2

CARING FOR POND PLANTS

WATERING WATER PLANTS
Once they are established in their permanent positions, of course, pond plants are unlikely to need watering, but it is important before planting to keep them moist by standing them in shallow water at all times. Also make sure that freshly planted baskets are thoroughly soaked with a fine-rosed watering can before immersion in the pond, to empty any pockets of air that might bubble up and disturb the contents

Planting and maintaining water plants is relatively simple compared with the needs of other garden species. It is easy to underestimate their adaptability, for many aquatic species will thrive at different depths and in various conditions. In general, pond plants are remarkably vigorous and robust, and more likely to need thinning or division to restrain their spread than any special encouragement to grow.

PLANTING

Two factors need bearing in mind when planting water aquatic species: the type of plant (see p48), and the time of year. The best seasons for introducing new plants are late spring and early summer, when active growth is under way and the water is starting to warm up. Try to complete the planting of hardy species by early summer to allow them time to establish fully before the water begins to cool in autumn, and finish with the tender or exotic plants that need frost-free conditions (see p64).

Methods of planting vary according to type. Floaters are launched on the pond surface, where they will drift freely and absorb nutrients from the water through their dangling roots, and need no more attention apart from occasional thinning should they multiply too vigorously.

Oxygenators, too, can be installed by simply tossing them into the water: they are normally supplied as bundles of unrooted cuttings, bound with a soft lead strip that causes them to sink to the bottom where they root without further attention. They may also be planted in soil or gravel where this covers the bottom of the pond or marginal shelf, using a brick or large stone to hold them in place while rooting. Alternatively, group several bunches in a planting basket filled with soil or gravel, spacing them evenly and planting fairly firmly.

The same choice – planting in containers or direct bottom planting – exists for water lilies and other deep water aquatics, and for marginal plants. Containers such as perforated baskets offer a number of advantages that simplify planting and subsequent care (see p52–3), especially in a small pond where they are easily accessible. In larger ponds and those with a soil bottom, direct planting is possible, either in the same way as for oxygenators or by submersing each plant in a weighted sack. In this case prepare enough planting medium (garden soil or special aquatic compost) to enclose the roots in a 20cm (8in) layer and place this rootball, together with a heavy stone, in the centre of a square piece of hessian sacking. Secure this loosely around the neck of the plant and then lower the small 'sack' into the water at the chosen position. There it will sink to the bottom, and the roots will push through the hessian into the soil.

PROPAGATION

Aquatic plants are no more difficult to multiply than their terrestrial relatives, and you do not need any special equipment to propagate extra plants and increase your stock or replace older plants that have become exhausted. The simplest method for many species is division, although some plants may also be propagated by taking cuttings or sowing seeds.

■ **Division** Water lilies are usually multiplied by dividing their creeping rhizomes with a sharp knife (see p53). The same principle applies to most deep water aquatics and marginals, all of which need thinning periodically. Dig up a large clump or remove it from its planting basket, then insert two garden forks back to back into the clump so that you can lever it in half – some plants are more easily cut with a knife or spade. Repeat this until you have enough healthy young segments for replanting. Discard the older exhausted part of the plant.

■ **Cuttings** A number of plants, especially creeping species such as brooklime and bogbean, can be grown from cuttings taken at any time during the growing season. Take a 5cm (2in) length from the end of a shoot, cutting just below a leaf. Remove the leaves from the lower portion of the stem. Dip the cut end in rooting hormone preparation and then insert up to the lowest leaves in a tray of mud. Keep the tray in a container of water until the cuttings are rooted.

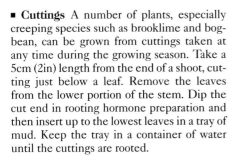

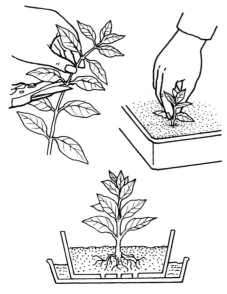

■ **Sowing** In addition to water lilies (see p76), many other species can be propagated from seeds, in most cases as soon as they are ripe in summer or early autumn – if you cannot sow immediately, store the seeds in a cup or tube of water. Sow in the normal way on the surface of moist seed compost or an aquatic mixture, and cover with a thin layer of sharp sand. Place the tray in shallow water

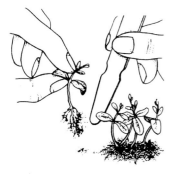

Prick out seedlings when the first true leaves develop

in another container. Stand this in shade, outdoors or inside, until seedlings appear, when the water level can then be increased to cover the seed tray. Prick out when the first true leaves develop.

●

WATER LILIES FROM EYES

Large numbers of new lilies can be raised at any time between late spring and late summer by separating dormant buds or 'eyes' from a mature plant. Use a sharp knife to remove them and dust the cut surfaces with sulphur to discourage fungal diseases. The eyes are then potted individually in small pots of clean garden soil or aquatic compost, and kept just submerged in a bowl of water; the adult rhizome can be replanted in the pond. Pot on the young plants until they are large enough to be planted in a basket or direct in the pond. Eyes take 2–3 years to make flowering size crowns.

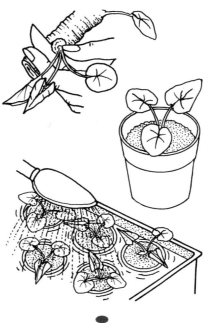

●

PLANTING SHELVES

Where possible try to incorporate marginal shelves around the sides of the pond, increasing in depth by 20–30cm (8–12in) stages and so providing different levels for various plant species to grow at their preferred depths. This arrangement also offers a choice of temperature zones for pond wildlife and a shallow safety area around the pond.

See also:
Dividing perennials (p41)
Dividing water lilies (p53)
Effective plant protection (p12)
Feeding plants (p40)
Gathering dormant buds (p103)
Insects and water plants (p64)
Introducing last plants (p64)
Monitoring overwintering plants (p21)
Overwintering a lotus (p115)
Overwintering water lilies (p115)
Planting aquatics (p52)
Planting in baskets (p52)
Planting water violets (p29)
Propagating shrubs (p129)
Protecting fragile plants (p114)
Renewing marginals (p29)
Sowing primulas (p41)
Thinning floaters (p76)
Tidying top growth (p102)
Top dressing water lilies (p29)
Water lilies from seed (p77)
Water lily care (p90)
Water plants in autumn (p114)

OCTOBER

Winter is still many weeks away, and the autumn tints of tree and shrub foliage may tempt you to pause and admire the visible beauty of hidden chemical changes inside the plants. But there is also a new menace in the air, with sudden gales stripping leaves from trees and dumping them in the pond, and perhaps even a light frost, the first for several months.

Life in the pond is winding down. Plants have been looking tired for a little while now, ever since the last water lilies faded and crumpled, and it is time to start seasonal tidying in earnest. There are seeds to gather, old dry stems to cut down, and weeds to pull out. Resist the temptation to clear away every dying leaf, though: many of the creatures that frequented the pond in summer will be looking for shelter now, and it is easy in your enthusiasm to deny them the hiding places they need to survive the winter unharmed.

As aquatic plants die back, vivid goldfish too will need to find alternative hideouts where they can lurk less conspicuously. They have not always sported the brilliant colours for which they are collected today – when their history began nearly 1700 years ago they were just slightly more interesting forms of the drab local Chinese carp. It was another millennium and many generations of careful selection before fancy variations in colour and shape became common, leading to their growing popularity, first throughout the Far East and then to Europe and North America.

For all their exotic beauty, most are very hardy and will withstand falling water temperatures, provided they are well nourished and in good shape. A little attention now to building up their strength for the winter and protecting them from predators will ensure their survival through the cold months ahead.

tasks

FOR THE

month

WATER PLANTS IN THE AUTUMN

Although some plants, mainly terrestrial and marginal species, need cutting back in autumn, most other water plants can be left to die down naturally.

■ **Deep water aquatics** – most decompose in the water and leave little trace behind apart from a greasy deposit on the surface

■ **Floating plants** – these tend to produce winter buds that sink to the bottom where they remain dormant until spring; the rest of the plant breaks up and sinks without trace

■ **Oxygenating plants** – some produce winter buds, while others make dormant crowns on the bottom or continue to function as normal during winter

■ **Bog plants** – cut back those near the water's edge, but leave others to decline naturally and use their foliage as a protective mulch over dormant crowns

CHECKLIST

- Protect the crowns of frost-shy plants
- Plant hardy perennials
- Prepare the sacred lotus for winter
- Plan and start extensions
- Continue clearing autumn leaves (see p102)

PROTECTING FRAGILE PLANTS

The first severe frosts may be a real threat soon, and as their foliage finally dies down this is a good time to tuck up the dormant crowns of frost-shy plants to protect them.

■ Despite its robust appearance, the giant rhubarb *(Gunnera manicata*, p117) is particularly sensitive to frost and should be protected with a thick tent of its own leaves or a good layer of bracken or conifer branches

■ Arum lilies *(Zantedeschia*, p116) also benefit from a cover of dead leaves or a wire netting enclosure stuffed with straw for insulation

■ Some more exotic species of *Cortaderia (Gynerium)* and *Pennisetum* should be mulched with bracken, leaves, straw or similar dry litter.

■ The water hyacinth *(Eichornia crassipes*, p14) should be removed from the pond and divided for storing in wet mud or moist pots under glass until the spring

PLANT BOG GARDEN PERENNIALS

Perennials can be planted in spring (see p41), but there are often many other jobs to do then, together with a risk that in a dry season spring introductions may need careful watering until they are established, even in the moist soils of the bog garden. Many gardeners favour autumn planting instead, when the soil is still warm and plants

have time to establish before becoming dormant for the winter. Many species can be planted at either time of year, although you should check details for specific species in the Plants of the Month pages as some prefer one or other season for a number of reasons. Much depends on the availability of new plants, but autumn planting is often easier because you can take more time over the job without any concern for the later care plants might need. Also existing plants can be divided or moved to

re-establish whole areas of the bog garden if these have been unsatisfactory during the past season. The planting method is the same as in spring (see p41).

OVERWINTERING A LOTUS

The East Indian or sacred lotus *(Nelumbo nucifera*, p131), is a tender plant normally grown in an indoor pond or planted outdoors for the summer. Plants grown under glass will overwinter safely, provided the water is kept from freezing, but outdoor specimens planted in ponds or tubs must be brought under cover in mid-autumn for storage. If grown in large baskets, these should be lifted out and the roots removed for storing in a box of damp sand; rhizomes planted directly into the soil need even greater care during lifting (they are extremely brittle) before storing in the same way in frost-free conditions. The

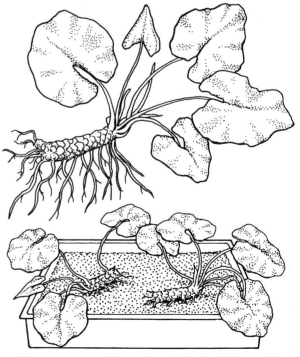

Lotus roots prepared for overwintering in a box of damp sand

rhizomes are divided in spring for replanting, making sure each root segment has two good buds.

It is worth noting that in temperate climates sacred lotus often receive insufficient sunlight for the rhizomes to survive the winter, and they may not be fit to re-use in the spring – for this reason many gardeners treat them as annuals, discarding them rather than attempting to overwinter the roots.

AN AUTUMN START TO NEW WORK

As with planting, autumn is an alternative time for starting new ponds or extensions to existing ones, free from the urgency of spring as the garden returns to life. Whether you are making a new pond or adding features such as a waterfall or artificial stream, conditions are usually still warm enough to make the work pleasant, while the risk of prolonged frost is still slight. This is a good time for laying concrete in any quantity because it needs to dry slowly, protected from hot sunshine, but it is equally at risk from hard frost and if this is forecast you should cover freshly laid concrete with sacking while it is still wet. Remember, too, that curing takes a day or two longer than in summer when temperatures are higher.

OVERWINTERING WATER LILIES

In deep ponds, water lilies will be safe below any ice during the winter and there is no need to take any special precautions. Where the water depth is less than about 45cm (18in), however, plants may suffer in colder districts and should be brought indoors for safety. Lift their containers from the pond, trim back any remaining leaves, and submerge them in containers of water in a frost-free greenhouse until the spring.

WATCH OUT FOR
Autumn stems and leaves
As leaves with their lovely tints fall from trees and shrubs, it is easy to think that autumn means a bleak end to colour around the pond. But with thoughtful planting, it is possible to have beauty of a different kind right through until spring.

■ **Shrubs** Grow shrubs with coloured stems: many willows (Salix), dogwoods (Cornus) and ornamental brambles such as the white-stemmed Rubus thibetanus (ghost bramble) revel in bog garden conditions and keep their colour all winter.

■ **Grasses** Even when their topgrowth has died, many grasses have a beauty of their own, sometimes soft and inviting like the blonde clumps of Pennisetum, and occasionally startling – the bizarre hairstyles of Oryzopsis (rice grass), for example, or the bold plumes of Cortaderia and Miscanthus.

■ **Trees** Small waterside trees with interesting networks of branches add form and drama to the winter pond. Try some of the small Prunus and Acer species, Styrax japonicum (Japanese snowbell) with its tracery of slim branches, or the permed effect of the Japanese larch, Larix kaempferi 'Diane', all suitable for planting beside ponds in small gardens.

plants
OF THE
month
1

ARUM LILY, CALLA LILY
(Zantedeschia aethiopica)

Perhaps more familiar as a potted houseplant, arum lilies are quite hardy if their crowns are protected by a mulch or minimum depth of water in winter. A well-grown clump is breath-taking in bloom.

type	Hardy or half-hardy deciduous or semi-evergreen perennial; bog or marginal plant
flowers	Tiny, on a fragrant yellow spike enclosed in a large white spathe, in spring and summer, sometimes followed by yellow or orange berries
foliage	Glossy and rich green, heart-shaped on long stalks
height	45–60cm (18–24in)
spread	30–38cm (12–15in)
position	Full sun or semi-shade, in moist soil in bog gardens, or at the edge of ponds in water, depth 5–30cm (2–12in)
planting	Spring, singly or 25cm (10in) apart in groups, direct into the soil or in buried pots, or in baskets for planting under water
care	In autumn cover terrestrial plants with a thick mulch of bracken, straw or leaves for protection; lift sunken pots and overwinter indoors. Unless submerged under at least 15–20cm (6–8in) of water, aquatic specimens should be lifted and stored under glass
propagation	Division in spring
related plants	The variety 'Crowborough' is hardier than most

GOAT'S BEARD
(Aruncus dioicus)

Elegant leaves and majestic flowers guarantee the popularity of this wild flower for shaded sites in larger bog gardens. It needs plenty of room, although a more compact variety is available.

type	Hardy herbaceous perennial; bog plant
flowers	Tiny and creamy white, on large fluffy flowerheads, in early and mid-summer
foliage	Fresh green, numerous deeply serrated leaflets arranged on a long stem
height	1.8m (6ft)
spread	90cm (3ft)
position	Light or medium shade, in rich, moist and leafy soil where the large plants can safely cast their own shade
planting	Autumn or spring, singly or 75cm (30in) apart in strategic groups, by the water
care	Mulch with compost in autumn, and feed with a general fertilizer in spring. Cut down all growth almost to ground level in late autumn
propagation	Division in autumn or spring
related plants	'Kneiffii' is similar but much smaller, only 60cm (2ft) high

WATER HAWTHORN
(Aponogeton distachyos)

An excellent choice for deep water ponds. Plants are easily grown and long flowering, especially in shade, with attractive floating leaves that are more or less evergreen; the exciting fragrance of the blooms is powerful and lingering.

type	Hardy semi-evergreen perennial; deep water aquatic

flowers	Strongly fragrant and white, with waxy petals and black anthers, in forked spikes that almost float on the surface; late spring and autumn or continuously in mild shade
foliage	Long, oval and mid-green with brown blotches, floating on the surface and evergreen in mild gardens
height	10cm (4in)
spread	90cm (3ft)
position	Full sun or partial shade in water, depth 30–90cm (12–36in)
planting	Spring, planting tubers or young plants 45cm (18in) apart, in small isolated groups direct into the soil or in baskets
care	Remove dead foliage as it appears. Plants survive the winter safely if their tubers are below the ice; otherwise overwinter baskets under cover, in damp sand and darkness
propagation	Ripe floating seeds sown in containers of water indoors in autumn; division in late spring

(GIANT) PRICKLY RHUBARB
(Gunnera manicata)

The essential plant for the largest ponds, perhaps the most magnificent of all and vast enough to shelter beneath. True to its exotic appearance it is not fully hardy and needs protection in cooler gardens.

type	Hardy or half-hardy herbaceous perennial; bog plant
flowers	Small and greenish red, massed on a stout cone-shaped spike up to 1.5m (5ft) high; late summer
foliage	Rich green, serrated and indented, 1.8–3m (6–10ft) across on strong prickly stalks
height	2–3m (6¹/₂–10ft)
spread	5m (16ft)
position	Full sun or semi-shade, in a warm site sheltered from cold winds and late frosts, in rich moist or wet soil beside large ponds
planting	Late spring, in wet soil that has been enriched with plenty of compost
care	Mulch around young growth in spring. Cut down faded flower stems, and in late autumn cut foliage and use to cover the crown for winter protection
propagation	Fresh seeds sown in autumn in a cold frame; division in spring
related plants	*G. tinctoria*, slightly smaller in size; *G. magellanica* is a miniature, only 10cm (4in) high and spreading to 90cm (3ft), for smaller ponds

practical project 1

MAKING WATER FLOW: 1

STREAMS

Moving water is a refreshing feature, contributing light and music to the garden, cooling the air and creating an atmosphere altogether different from that of still tranquil pools. It is an adaptable medium: a stream may be formal or informal, for example, a simple link between two ponds or a major feature in its own right, gently meandering through waterside plants or tumbling noisily over rocks and pebbles. The possibilities are infinite, especially if you combine flowing water with features such as fountains (p122) and waterfalls or cascades (p140). All you need is a submersible pump (see p87) or a natural source such as a spring to bring movement to the water garden.

NATURAL SOURCES

You might be lucky enough to have a natural spring in your garden, and this may be exploited to feed a water course. In the surrounding marshy soil you can plant a variety of bog and marginal species. On a slope, a header pool can be dug out and lined, to fill and create a reservoir that will feed a stream or waterfall leading the water wherever you would like it to flow. Springs may be seasonal, however, and your design and also choice of plants should take into account the possibility of a reduced flow or even drought in summer.

Similarly with natural streams, whose rate of flow can fluctuate widely according to the time of year and amounts of rainfall. Either leave an existing stream unimproved and simply plant suitable marginals in the banks and shallows, or carefully modify its course to feed a garden pond or flow over a cascade. Garden features should include an overflow and a topping up inlet to compensate for seasonal changes in the amount of water being delivered. Remember that you will not usually be allowed to alter the volume flowing from your garden downstream without permission from local authorities.

SITING AND MARKING OUT

In a fairly level garden it might be necessary to create a bank or slope before installing an artificial stream, using the soil excavated from the pond site to provide the extra height. The slope need not be steep; the chosen gradient will largely depend on the desired effect.

Plan the course so that it offers natural vari-ety: allowing it to meander gently, for example, will offer more sites for plants, while intro-ducing an abrupt change of level can provide opportunities for including a waterfall or cas-cade, or a series of small pools. For an informal design make sure the source, in particular, looks natural – the outlet of the delivery hose from a pump can be submerged in a header pool or hidden in a group of rocks. More for-mal streams can be fed from a stone ornament, a tilted urn or a pond with a small fountain.

Mark out in the same way as for a pond (see pp24–5), and then excavate the full length of the stream course according to whether you are making it from concrete, a flexible liner or preformed units (see p140). Take care to test the gradients of individual sections with a plank of wood and a spirit level: a simple stream needs a fairly consistent gradient, whereas intervening stretches within a series of connected pools or small waterfalls should be almost level. Check especially that the excavation is level across from one bank to the other to avoid lateral loss of water.

A CONCRETE STREAM COURSE

Concrete is a useful material for artificial streams and much easier to handle than when making a pond. The finish is not so critical and the final surface may be left roughly sculpted to develop a naturally weathered appearance. If you are laying concrete direct, make sure the banks are no steeper than about 45 degrees, otherwise shuttering will be needed to keep the mix in place.

■ Dig out the stream 13–15cm (5–6in) deeper than the final dimensions, and line the site with a 5cm (2in) layer of builder's sand.

■ Over this lay a standard concrete mix (see p33, Mix 2) about 8cm (3in) thick, starting from one end and spreading the concrete with a trowel from the bottom of the stream up the walls.

■ After a few hours, when the concrete has 'gone off', arrange any rocks in natural groups along the edges, pressing them firmly into the concrete. Stones or river gravel may also be added to the stream bed to vary the flow of the water.

■ Leave the concrete to dry slowly (see p32) and then replace any soil needed to finish the edges. Flush the stream thoroughly with water before adding plants.

Cross-section of concrete stream course

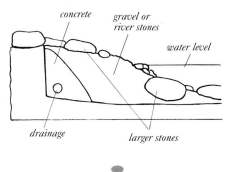

concrete

gravel or
river stones

water level

drainage

larger stones

USING A FLEXIBLE LINER

■ Excavate the stream course, allowing room for an underlining (see p44): make it 2.5cm (1in) deeper for material such as felt, 5cm (2in) deeper for a layer of sand.

■ Remove any sharp stones or roots, firm the soil and lay the underlining.

■ Calculate the amount of liner needed (see p56) and cut to size; add an extra margin of at least 8cm (3in) at each side for bedding into the bank (more if you plan for marginal bog plants), and cut separate pieces for individual pools or sections, allowing a 30cm (12in) overlap where pieces meet.

■ Spread the liner smoothly in the bed of the stream, overlapping sections in the direction of the flow of water and tucking the edges securely in the soil along the top of the banks.

■ Test the lie and gradient of the course by running water down the stream.

■ Stones may be added along the edges and on the stream bed, but use only well-rounded specimens to avoid puncturing the plastic.

FERNS FORSTEAMS

Many ferns enjoy cool moist sites and these can be incorporated into waterside planting schemes, especially in combination with primulas and irises. Choose species from genera such as:

Matteuccia, e.g. *M. struthiopteris* (ostrich plume fern)
Onoclea, e.g. *O. sensibilis* (sensitive fern)
Osmunda, e.g. *O. regalis* (royal fern)
Thelypteris (acid soils only), e.g. *T. palustris* (marsh fern).

TO CALCULATE THE LIKELY RATE OF FLOW

Multiply depth x width x length of the stream to give its water volume. The pump will have a given output, from which the speed can be worked out.

Example: if the water volume is 200 litres and the pump moves 200 litres/minute, the entire contents of the stream are circulated every minute. If the stream is 5m long, the water will flow at a rate of 4m/minute (1 litre occupies 1000cm³).

ADJUSTING WATER VELOCITY

Ensuring an adequate and convincing flow of water depends partly on the size of the pump: fitting a more powerful pump will increase the output of water at the source, which will either increase the rate of flow along the stream or allow you to build a wider stream bed.

This speed may be imperceptible. You can increase the flow by reducing the depth or width of the stream – halving either will double the flow. You can reduce the depth with a layer of gravel on the bottom, and the width by positioning stones within the stream bed.

Gradient, too, can affect the flow and the ideal fall for a stream ranges between 2.5–5cm/metre (1–2in/yard): the greater the fall, the faster the flow.

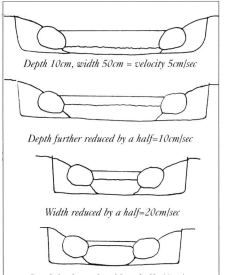

Depth 10cm, width 50cm = velocity 5cm/sec

Depth further reduced by a half=10cm/sec

Width reduced by a half=20cm/sec

Depth further reduced by a half=40cm/sec

NOTE
For fountains see pp122–3, for waterfalls see pp140–1.

plants

OF THE

month

2

FLOATING AQUATICS

Floating aquatic plants or 'floaters' are an important component of the balanced pond because they support the surface cover provided mainly by water lilies and deep water aquatics (see p48). Some form carpets of foliage that will need thinning occasionally (see p76), whereas many others, mainly larger leafed species, develop into separate floating clumps and may be left alone. Planting is simple: the plants are merely dropped into the water or placed on the surface. Most hardy forms multiply freely, at varying rates, and survive winters by sinking to the bottom as dormant seeds or buds. (See also Eichornia crassipes *and* Pistia stratiotes, *p14–15)*

BLADDERWORT
(Utricularia vulgaris)

An odd carnivorous plant, with leaves and stems that float just below the surface where their tiny swollen bladders catch and digest minute aquatic fauna. The pretty summer flowers seem to rise from the empty water.

flowers	Small, bright yellow or golden orange, pouched like small speckled antirrhinums, in late summer
foliage	Dark green, finely divided and thread-like, floating in tangled masses beneath the surface
height	23cm (9in)
spread	50sq cm (20sq in) per year
care	Occasionally needs thinning. Plants are hardy and survive winter as dormant buds on the bottom of the pond
propagation	Division of foliage in spring and summer
related plants	*U. minor* (Lesser Bladderwort) is smaller and more delicate, with pale yellow flowers. Many other similar species are sometimes available, but may not be hardy

DUCKWEED
(Lemna trisulca)

Introduce the wrong species of duckweed and the pond will soon be covered with a bright

green blanket (see p65). This is the only one that is safe to grow, for it is far less invasive and forms pretty mats of floating stars.

flowers	Tiny and insignificant
foliage	Minute translucent fronds like crisp stars, each with a single dangling root, forming small masses that float just below the surface
spread	0.5sq m (1.5 sq ft) per year or less
care	Thin occasionally if mats become too congested. Plants overwinter as dormant buds on the bottom of the pond
propagation	Redistribution of fronds
related plants	*L. gibba* (Thick Duckweed), *L. minor* (Common Duckweed), and *L. polyrhiza*, syn. *Spirodela polyrhiza* (Greater Duckweed) are all rapidly invasive and best avoided

FAIRY MOSS
(Azolla filiculoides, syn. *A. caroliniana)*

A charming tiny fern that congregates into dense masses in still water. Keeping this multiplication under control in a small pond is not a problem, but as plants can eventually cover the whole surface, you should not introduce this into large inaccessible ponds.

flowers	None
foliage	Pale blue-green lacy fronds, only 1cm (¹/₂in) across, turning rich reddish purple in autumn
height	2.5cm (1in)
spread	1sq m (3sq ft) per year
care	Trawl out unwanted plants with a net during the growing season. Plants survive winter as submerged dormant buds, but as frost injury is possible some plantlets should be overwintered under glass in a jar of water and soil
propagation	Plantlets redistributed on the surface in mid-spring

FROGBIT
(Hydrocharis morsus-ranae)

A restrained floater that is an ideal choice for smaller ponds. It resembles a miniature water lily, although the small pretty flowers are simpler and short-lived.

flowers	Small and white, three-petalled with bright yellow centres, on raised stalks; mid- and late summer

foliage	Dull bronze-green, small and kidney-shaped, arranged in rosettes that form on runners
height	2.5–5cm (1–2in)
spread	1sq m (3sq ft) per year
care	Plants may need thinning with a net in very small ponds. Dormant buds ('turions') normally overwinter safely on the bottom, but keep a few plantlets under glass in jars of water and soil as an insurance
propagation	Plantlets removed from the ends of runners at any time, or overwintered under glass and redistributed in mid-spring

WATER CHESTNUT
(Trapa natans)

This extremely decorative annual is a commercial crop in warmer climates. In cooler regions plants only flower if the summers are hot, and production of the edible nut-like fruits is uncertain. Well worth growing both outdoors and under glass, in a depth of 30cm (12in) of water.

flowers	Small, white and delicate, hidden among the foliage, in mid- to late summer, followed by spiny, hard black fruits, 2.5cm (1in) across
foliage	Dark green and shiny, angular and toothed, on the ends of inflated stems, arranged in rosettes that often root in shallow water.
height	2.5cm (1in)
spread	1sq m (3sq ft) per year
care	In warmer regions may be invasive and need thinning in summer. The annual plants are killed by autumn frosts, and need renewal each year unless fruits form and overwinter safely on the bottom of the pond
propagation	Fruits kept damp and frost-free over winter and dropped in the pond in spring; new young plants in spring

WATER SOLDIER
(Stratiotes aloides)

Semi-evergreen and usually described as resembling a floating pineapple top, this can be invasive but is easily controlled. Plants are attractive and interesting, rising and sinking again at different times during the season according to their growth stage. A good choice for wildlife ponds.

flowers	Separate male and female forms, small, creamy white and papery, tucked in the leaf axils; mid- to late summer
foliage	Dark olive-green, narrow and sharp, arranged in neat rosettes, often just below the surface when plants are not in flower
height	2.5–5cm (1–2in)
spread	1sq m (3sq ft) per year
care	Thin out occasionally with a net. The plants usually overwinter at the bottom of the pond, but a few may be kept indoors in jars of water and soil for redistribution in spring
propagation	Division of clumps in spring and summer

(clockwise from top right) Water soldier; water chestnut; fairy moss and frogbit

practical
project
2

MAKING WATER
FLOW: 2

FOUNTAINS

A fountain is the most animated moving water feature, one that complements formal and informal ponds equally well. Tall classic sprays are strongly compelling architectural statements, especially in grand formal settings, while, at the other end of the scale, small bubble jets and bell sprays harmonize with modern garden designs and make perfect diminutive fountains for mini-ponds and indoor use, or where young children are likely to be playing.

CHOOSING A FOUNTAIN

As suggested, it is vital that the chosen fountain should blend with the pond and the rest of the garden both in style and dimensions; fortunately there is a vast range of jets and sprays available to suit almost any setting, and the height of the jet is usually adjustable. Remember that a fountain is likely to be a focal point and should be set off to advantage – do not combine one with a waterfall or cascade, or any other strong feature as they will compete for attention.

All fountains work on the same principle: an electrically driven pump, either submersible or surface mounted (see p86), draws water from a pond or fountain basin through its filter assembly and drives it to the fountain head or jet through a delivery pipe of varying length. The size of pump must be matched with the volume of water to be delivered, which in turn depends on the number of jets and the height of desired spray.

Although a fountain is a compelling ornament in its own right, the display can be enhanced by adding subtle lighting from underwater spotlights (see p107), and rotating or repeating devices that automatically produce a sequence of changing spray patterns. These are most suitable for larger fountains in very formal settings. Avoid siting any fountain near to trees and other large structures and try to position it so that it has a well-lit background – good light increases the sparkle of the spray.

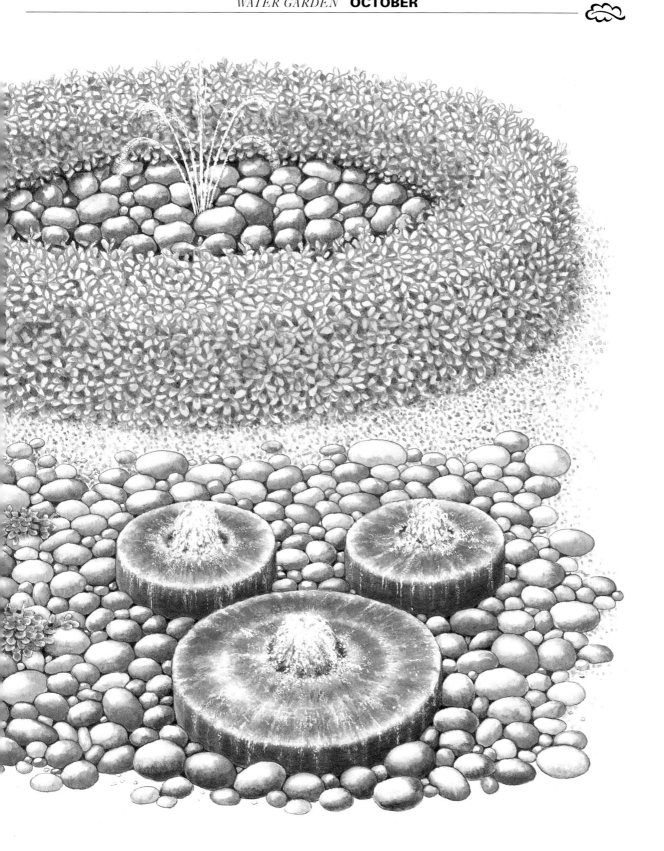

practical
project
2

MAKING WATER
FLOW: 2
continued

TYPES OF JET

Bell A uniform hemisphere of water, the best kind for avoiding damage to nearby aquatic plants.

Bubble An adjustable head of gently bubbling water ideal for millstones and pebble fountains.

Geyser Taller than a bubble jet, with a gushing stream of foamy water.

Spray Single or multiple jets producing an arching spray of water falling in a circle.

Tier A more elaborate spray rising in a series of diminishing circular layers.

Tulip Variation on the bell jet, equally neat but with an open centred stem.

THE MECHANICS OF FOUNTAINS

- *The wider the hose, the better: water travels faster in a 2.5cm (1in) diameter hosepipe than 1cm ('/in) tubing.*
- *Keep the delivery hose straight and as short as possible to reduce friction.*
- *To look in proportion, the spray height should be less than half the width of the pond.*
- *Submerging the end of the outlet pipe can determine the type of spray produced. The closer the pipe is to the surface the thinner and taller the spray will be.*
- *Very fine sprays drift in the breeze and are less conspicuous than coarser ones.*
- *Submersible pumps are adequate for most purposes, but for multiple jets or sprays much above 3m (10ft) a surface mounted mains pump is advisable.*
- *Small fountains 1.2m (4ft) high or less can often be operated by low voltage pumps.*

A SIMPLE FOUNTAIN

- If you are using a surface pump, a dry chamber must be built near to the pond (see p86).

- In small ponds it is usual to connect the spray jet direct to the outlet on the top of the pump body – stand the pump on bricks stacked to raise the jet to the required height (protect liners with a square of carpet before positioning bricks).

- In larger ponds the fountain may be a long

way from the side, and the fountain jet should then be stood securely in position, coupled by a delivery pipe to the pump which is set near the pond edge on an underwater slab plinth to keep the filter clear of silt.

- Secure the electrical cable well out of the way and connect safely to the mains.

MILLSTONE FOUNTAINS

Natural or artificial millstones are very popular for making small bubble fountains that take up very little room. Although a simple device, the weight of the stone means that strong support is vital so construction of the fountain needs care. Stout welded wire mesh is ideal and can be set across the top of a buried water tank or on the marginal shelf of a circular excavation fitted with flexible pond line. Make sure the stone is absolutely level so that water flows evenly over its surface. The pump, output about 450 litres/hr (100 gal/hr), is set in the chamber with the bubble jet positioned in the central hole of the stone – feed the electricity cable out at one side. Surround the stone with cobbles to cover the mesh and cable.

PEBBLE FOUNTAINS

A pebble or cobble fountain is constructed in a similar way to a millstone fountain and uses a pump of comparable rating. However, there is greater flexibility in the choice of jet, and bubble, bell and geyser sprays are all equally attractive. For the chamber you can use a half-barrel or tub, either buried to its rim below ground or standing on the surface – treat the inside of wooden barrels as described on p94. If buried, the circle of mesh can rest on the

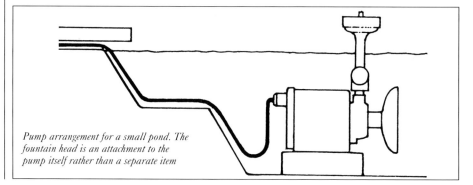

Pump arrangement for a small pond. The fountain head is an attachment to the pump itself rather than a separate item

rim; small free-standing containers can be filled completely with large pebbles, but half-barrels are best fitted with timber battens about 10–15cm (4–6in) below the rim to support the mesh. One or two pots of decorative grasses or sedges can be buried in the pebbles near the edge of the container to complete the project.

INSTALLING A WALL FOUNTAIN

Wall-mounted spouts, taps and gargoyles are the simplest fountains for limited space. The stream of water they produce can be caught in raised or sunken basins or small ponds, or, with a longer delivery pipe, it may be ducted to feed a series of miniature waterfalls and end in a reservoir in which the pump is housed, but make sure the pump is strong enough to lift water the greater distance to the outlet height on the wall.

There are several ways to install the delivery pipe, depending on the construction of the wall: holes can be drilled in the outer skin of a cavity wall so that the pipe may be fed in the lower hole, up through the cavity and out again at the back of the fountain. With a solid wall, either lead the pipe inside and out again at the top, or clip it to the outside with plumber's fastenings and disguise it with a length of ornamental drainpipe.

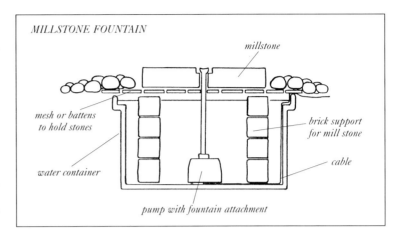

MILLSTONE FOUNTAIN

millstone

mesh or battens
to hold stones

brick support
for mill stone

water container

cable

pump with fountain attachment

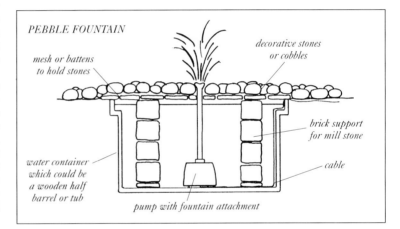

PEBBLE FOUNTAIN

decorative stones
or cobbles

mesh or battens
to hold stones

brick support
for mill stone

water container
which could be
a wooden half
barrel or tub

cable

pump with fountain attachment

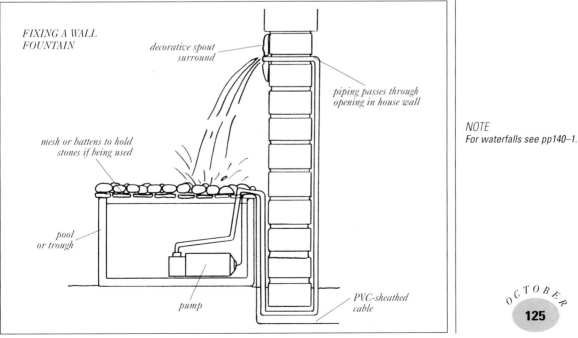

FIXING A WALL
FOUNTAIN

decorative spout
surround

piping passes through
opening in house wall

mesh or battens to hold
stones if being used

pool
or trough

pump

PVC-sheathed
cable

NOTE
For waterfalls see pp140–1.

NOVEMBER

Whether this month bids a last lingering farewell to autumn or heralds
the harsh arrival of winter is an annual gamble. Sometimes benign
weather holds on, soothing us into a dreamy lack of caution that can
be rudely repaid by a sudden and savage frost catching us unprepared.
Prudent gardeners take precautions this late in the season, tucking up
vulnerable plants with snug mulches of leaves or bracken to shield
their dormant crowns from cold. Tender aquatics or rooting portions
of them can be transferred to their winter quarters, in trays in a
greenhouse or submerged in the safety of an indoor pool. Whereas an
indoor pool might have seemed an ornamental extravagance at the
height of summer, its value is now apparent as a warm sanctuary for
frost-shy plants and less hardy fish.

If an outdoor pond is well-balanced and maintained with a diverse
population of flora and fauna, it should provide a sound habitat for
all seasons. But even the best-kept pond eventually starts to silt up
with soil and the debris of dead plants, so that a thorough overhaul
becomes necessary. This can be done either on a pleasant spring day
before plant growth revives, or now when floating plants need thinning
and autumn leaves have all fallen but not yet started to decay.

In a true wildlife pond, wholesale clearance would be too disruptive to
contemplate now, when the remains of summer plants have added to
the rich layer of organic litter on the bottom. Here many invertebrate
larvae and dormant plant buds have already settled in for the next
few months, secure against the hazards of winter, and it is best not to
disturb them.

tasks

FOR THE

month

CHECKLIST

- ☐ Prepare sinks and tubs for winter
- ☐ Stop feeding fish as temperatures fall
- ☐ Overhaul and store pumps and other equipment
- ☐ Take hardwood cuttings of pondside shrubs
- ☐ Finish protecting marginal plants for winter (see p112)

WINTER CARE OF MINI-PONDS

Tubs, sinks and other small water gardens need special preparation for winter, because they are exposed on all sides and their plants are more vulnerable to frost in such a small volume of water. Tropical water lilies and lotus can be allowed to die down for storage (see p115) or may simply be transferred to an indoor pond where they will continue growing if the surroundings are warm and the water kept well above freezing.

Other hardy plants can be left in a tub if you drain out the water to leave the bottom mud and then protect the container from frost: wrap bubble polythene insulation all around the outside and cover the mud inside with plenty of straw, bracken or similar protective material. In a dry winter check occasionally that

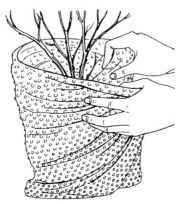

the mud is still moist. Pot up marginal plants; if they are already in containers, lift these out and then keep them in shallow water in a frost-free place.

CHECKING EQUIPMENT

If you have a pump powering a waterfall, fountain or filtration system, it should be disconnected now that frost is a possibility. Remove submersible pumps from the water, empty the pump chamber and wash out any sediment, and then clean and dry the working parts according to the manufacturer's instructions (always keep these because a simple annual servicing at this time of year will prolong the life of your equipment). In most cases the metal parts should be smeared with a film of grease before you store the pump in a dry place. Disconnect hoses and suction pipes, empty these out and store.

If you have installed a cistern and ballcock for automatically topping up the pond, this will need to be drained out to prevent frost damage; remember to connect a length of flexible hose between the pond inlet/outlet and the overflow to bypass the cistern during winter and to drain surplus water from the pond after heavy rain. Finally, check over the floating

pond heater and connect this ready for use.

MAKING A LEAF STACK

You will need to continue clearing away autumn leaves as they fall or drift near the pond. Where there are large quantities, do not burn them: if stacked to decay, they produce valuable leafmould which makes an excellent mulch and soil conditioner for a bog garden.

■ Make a square or cylindrical container from 90cm (3ft) high wire netting with a fine mesh (about 2.5cm (1in) is ideal), and secure this upright to a stake

■ Pack the leaves into this, firming or treading them into a solid mass. They are best gathered wet; dry leaves should be soaked for more efficient compaction

■ Leave the stack undisturbed until next autumn, when the contents will be crumbly and perfect for use around the garden; the container can be emptied in time for the new season's leaf-fall

■ Instead of turning them into leafmould, you can use fresh fallen leaves for protecting sensitive plants: heap them over each dormant crown and cover with fine plastic netting to prevent their blowing away.

PROPAGATING SHRUBS

Many waterside shrubs can be propagated at this time of year by rooting hardwood cuttings in a spare part of the garden.

■ Cuttings are prepared from vigorous new shoots that have plenty of healthy buds and are turning woody at the base

■ Trim each shoot to about 23–30cm (9–12in) long by cutting off the soft tip just above a bud and trimming the bottom below a bud

■ Make a V-shaped slot or narrow trench in the ground and line this with sharp sand

■ Insert the cuttings to leave

the top one-third exposed above the surface, refill the trench with soil and firm well

■ Alternatively, place the cuttings in pots of rooting compost and stand in a coldframe

■ Outdoor cuttings will have rooted by next autumn, those in frames by late spring or early summer, and may then be lined out in a nursery bed or transferred to permanent poolside homes

FEEDING FISH

All fish species are very sensitive to temperature changes, which is why great care must be taken when introducing them to a new pond in spring. At this time of year their metabolism is slowing down in tune with decreasing temperatures.

Supplementary high-protein feeding over the past two months will have built up their strength for facing winter, but sometime soon the gradually cooling water will finally reach 5°C (41°F), the critical point below which feeding should cease.

Remember to provide one or two 10cm (4in) diameter drain pipes on the bottom where fish can hide from predators now that all surface cover from floating plants has disappeared, and make sure the pond does not freeze over completely for any length of time in a prolonged cold snap (see p12).

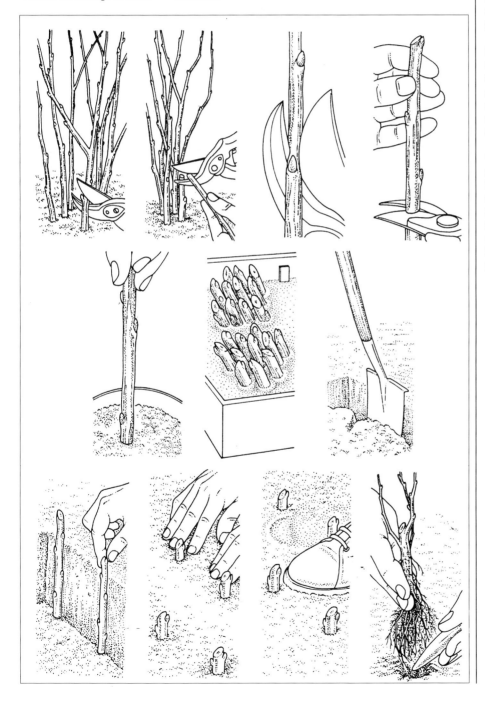

plants
OF THE
month

SWEET FLAG
(Acorus calamus)

A popular foliage plant, looking like an iris but not in any way related. Usually grown in its variegated form, with cream-striped leaves that smell of tangerines when crushed.

type	Hardy herbaceous perennial; marginal plant
flowers	Insignificant; small yellow spikes in early summer
foliage	Long and narrow, iris-like, with a conspicuous mid-rib, bright green or variegated
height	60–90cm (2–3ft)
spread	75cm (30in)
position	Full sun or very light shade, in wet soil or in water, depth 0–15cm (0–6in)
planting	Spring, 45cm (18in) apart, in bold groups, directly into the soil
care	Cut down dead foliage in late autumn or spring. Divide every 3–4 years
propagation	Division of rhizomes in spring
related plants	'Variegatus' is the most popular variety. *A. gramineus* is smaller, only 30cm (12in) tall, with a good striped form, 'Variegatus'

ROYAL FERN
(Osmunda regalis)

Perhaps the most impressive of all the hardy ferns (for others, see p117), once common in the wild and a desirable plant for large pond and streamside situations. Very vigorous and spreading, although some of the cultivated forms are less demanding of space.

type	Hardy deciduous fern; bog plant
flowers	Foliage plant only
foliage	Lime-green prettily divided fronds, first appearing as coppery crooked shoots and finally turning yellow and bronze in the autumn; smaller stiff spore-bearing fronds in the centre of plants
height	Up to 2.1m (7ft)
spread	1.8m (6ft)
position	Full sun, or light or moderate shade, in wet *acid* soils with plenty of humus, in larger bog gardens
planting	Spring, singly as large specimen plants, in lime-free soils fortified with plenty of leafmould or garden compost

care	Mulch with garden compost in spring and feed with a general fertilizer. Cover the crown with its dead fronds in late autumn for winter protection
propagation	Ripe spores surface-sown under glass in autumn or spring; division in spring
related plants	'Purpurascens' has purple-green fronds, while 'Cristata' and *undulata* are smaller plants with attractively tasselled foliage

EAST INDIAN LOTUS
(Nelumbo nucifera)

There are several gorgeous members of the lotus family. All are slightly tender in temperate gardens and therefore only suitable for planting outdoors in summer or for cultivation in large indoor ponds. This is one of the most spectacular.

type	Half-hardy herbaceous perennial; deep water aquatic
flowers	Pink, chalice-shaped with satiny petals and a fat central ovary, and very large, 30cm (12in) across, rising above the foliage; early summer to late autumn
foliage	Large, waxy and blue-green, like plates, at first floating and then held high above the water on long stalks
height	1.8m (6ft)
spread	2.1m (7ft)
position	Full sun, in a warm sheltered site, indoors or in baskets outdoors in summer only, in water, depth 30–60cm (12–24in)
planting	Late spring, burying the fragile rhizomes 10cm (4in) deep in well-

manured soil in large containers, which are then submerged

care	Feed with a water lily fertilizer every two months during the growing period. Rhizomes can survive winters outdoors if buried well below possible freezing levels; otherwise house baskets under glass in mid-autumn in damp sand
propagation	Division in spring in the same way as for water lilies, keeping at least two good buds on each segment of the creeping rhizome
related plants	Good varieties include 'Alba Grandiflora' (white), 'Alba Striata' (red-edged white), 'Pekinensis Rubra' (carmine); *N. lutea* 'Flavescens' is a smaller, yellow-flowered lotus, hardier than the others

KAFFIR LILY, RIVER LILY
(Schyzostylis coccinea)

A streamside plant in the wild, and useful for similar sites at the edge of ponds and running water. The simple species is beautiful but may soon form huge clumps, whereas cultivated forms are more restrained with larger blooms.

type	Hardy or half-hardy herbaceous perennial; bog and marginal plant
flowers	Open and star-shaped, arranged on spikes like a miniature gladiolus, pale or bright pink; mid-autumn to early winter
foliage	Mid-green, long, narrow and grassy, in vigorous clumps
height	60cm (2ft)
spread	25–30cm (10–12in)
position	Full sun with shelter from severe frosts, in moist or wet soil, and in shallow water, depth 0–10cm (0–4in)
planting	Spring, 25cm (10in) apart, in groups
care	Mulch in autumn and feed in spring with a general fertilizer. In very cold gardens cover crowns in winter with bracken or straw. Divide every 3–4 years, as the plants root freely and soon make a mat of thick roots with fewer flowers; replant in fresh soil
propagation	Division in spring
related plants	Named varieties include *alba*, 'Jennifer' (large, pink), 'Major' (rich red), 'November Cheer' (soft pink), 'Professor Barnard' (dark red), 'Sunrise' (salmon-pink)

practical project

BUILDING AN INDOOR POND

ADVANTAGES OF A RAISED POOL

- Contents closer to eye-level and more readily appreciated
- Planting and routine maintenance less arduous
- Safer if small children are about
- Less excavation needed during construction
- Water more easily siphoned out for cleaning

If you have a longing to grow water hyacinths to perfection or keep some of the fancier kinds of goldfish and shubunkins, an indoor pool can be the perfect solution to the problem of frosty winters outside. There are several different temperature regimes you can adopt for a greenhouse or conservatory (see box), depending on the amount of heating you are able or prepared to install. All offer the chance to keep a wider range of plants or fish, from overwintering tender aquatics in a frost-free environment to cultivating tropical water lilies and exotic fish (see p61) in a heated pool.

HEATING NEEDS AND COSTS

Conditions	Min winter temp	Cost
■ Cool (frost-free)	4°C (40°F)	C
■ Temperate	10°C (50°F)	2¥ C
■ Warm	15°C (60°F)	5¥ C

(C = the cost of maintaining frost-free conditions)
Double or triple glazing throughout can halve the value of C.

A lean-to structure attached to your house is ideal because the wall will trap and reflect solar heat, while some domestic heat will also increase the temperature of the glasshouse. Whatever the structure you choose, you will need to ensure adequate ventilation, shading to prevent scorch from direct sunlight, and a ready source of water for topping up the pool levels in summer. In return the whole greenhouse or conservatory will benefit from enhanced humidity levels produced by evaporation from the pond, and you will gain an attractive feature, either sunk in the ground (see p44) if it is to be part of a larger planting scheme, or raised to a more comfortable height for maximum convenience and enjoyment. Flexible liners and concrete are suitable materials, but the simplest method is to use a preformed shell (see p45).

CONSTRUCTING A RAISED POND

■ A raised rigid shell needs to be enclosed in a sturdy framework for support. This may be built from strong timber, minimum cross-section 15x10cm (6x4in) and half-lapped at the corners. Make the overall dimensions 15cm (6in) greater each way than the liner, and about 5–8cm (2–3in) higher from the ground.

■ A brick-built surround is stronger and can be more attractive. You can lay courses of bricks direct on a hard-surfaced floor, but if there is a soil base you will first need to construct a level concrete raft 15cm (6in) thick over the whole pond and wall area, and leave this for 1–2 weeks to cure. Measure an area 25cm (10in) longer and wider than the shell, and start building the walls two bricks thick, tieing the courses at intervals and finishing at the top with a course of coping stones or bricks on edge.

■ Rigid shells must be bedded on a layer of damp builder's sand spread 5cm (2in) thick over the floor of the structure. Centre the shell on this and support any irregular areas with large stones or bricks so that the unit is stable. Add about 15cm (6in) of water to steady the shell and then fill the space between this and the walls with sand, gravel or soil (see p45), finishing with 20cm (8in) of good topsoil or potting compost if you are adding edging plants.

■ If you decide to use a flexible plastic liner, stop building the walls one course below the top and line the structure with a backing of fleece or old carpet, securing this temporarily around the edges with coping stones or bricks. Calculate how much liner you need (see p56) and lay this inside the structure; pleat the corners neatly and trap the edges under the loose top course. Run in the water, smoothing out any wrinkles as the pond fills, and then mortar the top course to secure liner and backing in place.

■ Alternatively the completed brick walls can be rendered with waterproof mortar, smoothly skimmed with a plasterer's trowel or float, and finished with two coats of sealant or waterproof paint.

ESSENTIAL ACCESSORIES

A greenhouse or conservatory has a special microclimate, with a wide range of temperatures (sometimes very high) and strong light conditions. Combined with the small volume of water in the pond, these make water filtration essential (see p73) to maintain a clean habitat for fish. Aeration is also important for their good health: a small waterfall or bubble fountain will achieve this as well as enhancing the impact of the pond, but remember that water lilies do not like moving water. A further useful accessory is a water level monitor and automatic inlet for topping up the sometimes considerable losses from evaporation.

CONSTRUCTING A RAISED POND

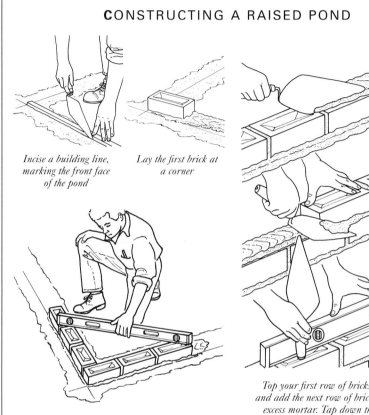

Incise a building line, marking the front face of the pond

Lay the first brick at a corner

Lay a few bricks (with the dips at the top) along both arms

Top your first row of bricks with mortar and add the next row of bricks, scraping off excess mortar. Tap down the bricks with the end of the trowel and use a spirit level to check for accuracy

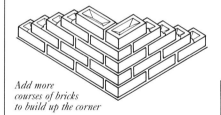

Add more courses of bricks to build up the corner

Work the opposite corner in the same way then complete the wall using a guideline of peg and twines to ensure the courses are level. The second (inner) leaf of bricks can be built up simultaneously. The two leaves need to be tied at regular intervals using metal butterfly ties

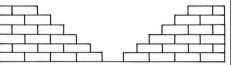

Remember to make frequent checks on alignment

HOUSEPLANTS FOR INDOOR PONDS

Heating a greenhouse allows you to grow plants from warmer aquatic environments. Here are a few of the more common genera, listed according to temperature regime, that appreciate high humidity and complement an indoor pond – they include climbers, ferns and foliage plants.

TEMPERATE HOUSE
Agapanthus, Alocasia, Asplenium, Brugmansia, Callistemon, Crossandra, Cryptanthus, Cyperus, Fatsia, Feijoa, Grevillea, Hibiscus, Hoya, Leucodendron, Ludwigia, Mandevilla, Monstera, Myriophyllum, Nephrolepis, Odontoglossum, Pilea, Sasa, Sorghum, Sparmannia, Strelitzia, Thalia, Zantedeschia

WARM HOUSE
Alternanthera, Anthurium, Caladium, Calathea, Chamaedorea, Chlorophytum, Clerodendron, Columnea, Cordyline, Dracaena, Episcia, Guzmania (and other bromeliads), *Hypoestes, Impatiens* (New Guinea types), *Maranta, Nepenthes* (and other carnivorous plants), *Plumeria, Salvinia, Schefflera, Spathiphyllum*

AQUATIC PLANTS FOR INDOOR PONDS

Cyperus involucratus (p15)
Eichornia crassipes (p14)
Nelumbo spp and vars (p131)
Nymphaea spp and vars (p70)
Pistia stratiotes (p15)

DECEMBER

In summer the floating zone of a pond is the most varied and lively ecosystem, the scene of rapid and dramatic increases in plant and animal populations. By contrast, the pond bottom is the place where everything happens in winter.

Even when the surface is sealed off with a thick layer of ice, microscopic creatures in the dark muddy ooze are breaking down organic materials into their valuable chemical constituents. The surface may be frozen quite often this month, which can be beneficial in some respects, because a ceiling of ice protects the water below from further heat loss unless the cold conditions persist for a long time. What might seem from above to be a frozen world, suspended in time, can be deceptive. In the chilly waters below, some submerged plants continue to live, their normal metabolic processes supplying oxygen for overwintering pond creatures. Only when ice exceeds about 5cm (2in) in thickness does it reduce the amount of light reaching plants in the depths. A covering of snow, on the other hand, seriously limits the passage of light and it is a good idea to sweep deposits from the frozen surface wherever possible.

This is a good time to assess the impact of your pond, while visible life is at a low ebb. One of the most important design considerations is a pond's appearance at all seasons of the year. Even in winter it is usually an important focus, its shape and proportions revealed for all to see. An imaginative choice of plants, with bold dramatic shapes and visual interest out of season, will pay dividends this month when conspicuous winter highlights are particularly reassuring and restore confidence in the promise of revival before many more weeks elapse.

tasks

FOR THE

month

DREAMING AND PLANNING
Planning a complete new water garden, or simply an extension or addition to an existing one, is almost as fascinating as the finished reality. At the preliminary stage all things seem possible, and it is important to temper ambition with an understanding of fundamental practical constraints (see p16). Nonetheless, this is the time of year to dream, when the pond is quiet and you have the leisure to decide the kind of water garden you would like – whether you want formality, fish and fountains, or perhaps to re-create a natural pond or running watercourse with all its teeming variety of flora and fauna, or simply make a mini-pond with a dwarf water lily or two.

If you already have a pond, maybe there is space to build a rock garden, bog garden or waterfall as an attractive extension, to bring it to life or set in context. The various projects in this book explain how to achieve a number of different styles and features.As another year in the water garden draws to a close, it is worth reflecting that there are many moods and unexpected pleasures impossible in a garden without water.

CHECKLIST

- [ ] Plan a continuous show of waterside flowers
- [ ] Consider what might have gone wrong this season
- [ ] Save time and effort with heavy mulching
- [ ] Plant trees and shrubs while dormant

PLANNING FOR COLOUR

Many of us would like a long sequence of colour from our pondside plants, and it is worth deciding at an early stage whether you would like your display to extend from spring until leaf-fall, or all the year round, which for most gardeners would be the ideal.

For **winter** interest, see p115. **Spring** is rarely a problem, colour appearing very early with the catkins of willow and hazel, followed quickly by the first primulas (p92), *Lysichitum* (p43), *Peltiphyllum* (p30) and various spring bulbs, culminating in the main spring display that is usually heralded by the yellow goblets of the marsh marigold, *Caltha palustris* (p42).

Summer is a green month, when a typical pond is surrounded by lush vegetation in all shapes and sizes. Colour highlights at this time include the globe flower *Trollius* (p54), astilbes (p79), mimulus (p108), *Lobelia cardinalis* (p104), day lilies (p66) and various irises (pp96 and 104).

Some of these continue well into **autumn**, although this season has its own treasures, such as hemp agrimony (p108) and dramatic *Ligularia dentata* (p109), brilliant river lilies *(Schizostylis)* (p131) and the curiously erratic water hawthorn, *Aponogeton* (p116). The changing colours of grasses, ferns and tree leaves link this season imperceptibly with winter once more.

GETTING THINGS RIGHT

As with any other form of gardening, there will be failures and success in the water garden over a single year. Problems are limited and rarely serious though, for the pond is a self-sustaining and self-regulating biotope (a specialized environmental unit), and when analysed most difficulties can be traced back to an early oversight in one of these key areas.

■ **Sound construction** – if the pond is carefully planned and properly built, little should go wrong

■ **Keeping it simple** – do not try to include every kind of feature or grow all the possible plant species, and do not mix ornamental fish with wildlife fauna

■ **Maintaining a balance** – keeping to recommended stocking rates for plants and fishes, and introducing them when conditions are right can prevent many basic problems

■ **Routine care** – looking after a pond is not arduous or demanding, but neglecting necessary tasks at particular times may lead to difficulties

■ **Regular inspection** – this should be a pleasure rather than a chore. Diseases sometimes occur, but prompt identification and treatment can help to avoid distress or loss

MULCHING MOIST AREAS

Bog gardens, especially larger ones, are difficult to keep weed-free at the best of times, but the problem is made worse by the inadvisability of using weedkillers so near to water. The cautious use of systemic herbicides during the preliminary clearance before construction will make for lighter work later, but weeds do arrive sooner or later. One effective method of suppressing them or preventing their establishment is to mulch the whole area very thickly – this will only work if you have larger plants, because mulching smothers low mat-forming or ground-cover plants unless applied carefully.

One of the best (and least expensive) materials is straw, which can be bought by the bale or trailer-load for spreading at this time of year when the bog garden is more accessible; it is pleasant work, too, for a cold early winter's day. Spread it evenly and thickly, 10–15cm (4–6in) deep, over the whole area including the dormant herbaceous plants – when these start growing again, they will push up through it in spring with little difficulty.

Next spring topdress all the plants with sulphate of ammonia, or dried blood if you are organic, which provides a supply of nitrogen to help break down the straw and feed the plants' growth: any form of carbon such as straw robs the soil of nitrogen as it decomposes, and this could lead to a shortage just when the plants need it. If you want to add more plants, simply push the straw aside, work a little fertilizer into the soil beneath and then plant as normal, finally tucking the straw back round the new plant. The mulch will gradually decay and improve the soil; you should not have to replace all the straw annually, however, but merely top it up to full depth again.

PLANTING TREES AND SHRUBS

Evergreen shrubs and trees are best planted in early autumn for easy establishment, but failing that (and always on cold heavy soils), they can be introduced in late spring. Deciduous

species are planted while dormant, any time between late autumn and early spring – here, too, autumn and early winter are the best times because the possible need for watering and other summer attention is reduced. Even container-grown plants, in theory capable of being planted at any time, succeed with the least attention if planted now.

■ Dig out a hole about twice the size of the rootball, and mix plenty of leafmould or tree planting compost into the well-broken excavated soil (1)

■ If a supporting stake is necessary, drive it in firmly at this stage (2)

■ Backfill the hole until it is the same depth as the container or, if the plant is bare-root, until the stem is at the same level as the old soil mark

■ Remove the container, if there is one, and loosen some of the roots

■ Hold the plant upright and half fill around the roots; firm this gently before filling the hole to the top (3)

■ Firm again, then loosen the surface and level. At this time of year, especially in bog gardens, no watering should be necessary (4)

■ Tie trees securely to their stakes with adjustable straps

BEDDING FOR PONDS

Instead of hardy perennials you might prefer to grow decorative annual bedding around your pond, depending on its situation. Most summer bedding plants are chosen for hot dry sites, but some of those species that do well in shade or in wet seasons would be appropriate choices for waterside planting.

Annuals for shade: begonias, calceolaria, campanula, coleus, fuchsias, impatiens, kochia, lobelia, mimulus, nemophila, nicotiana, pansies, stocks, violas

Annuals for moist positions: alyssum, antirrhinum, balsam, begonias, cineraria, dahlias, fuchsias, impatiens, lobelia, French marigolds, nemophila, phacelia, phlox, salvias, tagetes, violas

WATCH OUT FOR
Slippery paths and stepping stones
Various access areas such as stepping stones, bridges and waterside decking can become very slippery at this time of year, with shade and constant moisture encouraging the growth of algae and slime. Look out for the first signs of a greasy surface, and promptly scrub stonework with a stiff scrubbing brush and warm water. Timber surfaces should be covered with fine mesh netting nailed securely in place, or in summer when they are thoroughly dry they can be painted with a mixture of weatherproof adhesive and sand.

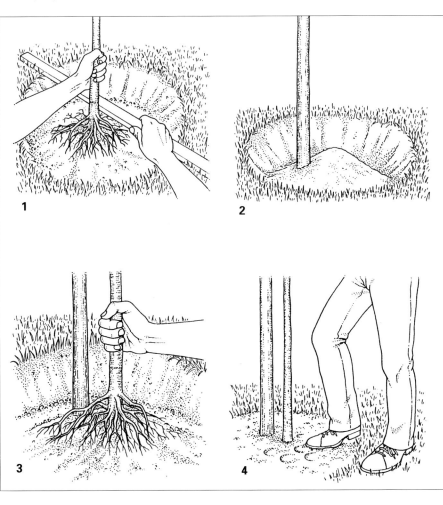

1

2

3

4

plants
OF THE
month

GRASSES, RUSHES AND SEDGES

To the inexperienced eye these are all very similar, and although botanically they are quite distinct, there is some virtue in grouping them together here. Many are grown as foliage plants, sometimes as ground cover, and can be very satisfying visually, offering a grace and elegance that other plants lack. Most are deciduous, dying back to ground level in winter, and a few have attractive flowers, although this is usually a bonus. Choose carefully: some can be undeniably invasive in moist situations, although the ornamental kinds selected here are more likely to behave themselves, especially if planted in baskets, and should need division only after several years.

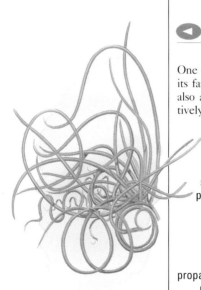

◄ CORKSCREW RUSH
(Juncus effusus 'Spiralis'*)*

One of nature's oddities and very popular for its fascinating contorted stems, although it is also a useful plant, its tenacious roots effectively stabilizing pond banks.

type	Hardy evergreen perennial rush; bog and marginal plant, and shallow water aquatic
height	45cm (18in)
spread	60cm (2ft)
position	Full sun or light shade, in very wet soil or in shallow water, depth 0–10cm (0–4in)
care	Plant in spring, 23cm (9in) apart in groups. In spring mulch or feed with a general fertilizer
propagation	Division in spring, every 4–5 years
related plants	*J. ensifolius*, flattened leaves and large dark brown flowers

STRIPED CLUB RUSH
(Schoenoplectus lacustris subsp. *tabernaemontani)*

Sometimes still found under its old name *Scirpus*, the variegated forms of this subspecies of true bulrush or plaiting rush are striking and popular foliage plants for larger natural ponds, equally dramatic when kept in containers in formal pools.

type	Hardy herbaceous perennial rush; bog and marginal plant, and shallow water aquatic
height	1.2–1.5 (4–5ft)
spread	60cm (2ft)
position	Full sun or light shade, in moist bog gardens and in water, depth 0–30cm (0–12in)
care	Plant in spring, singly or 30cm (12in) apart in small groups, and feed every spring with a general fertilizer
propagation	Division in spring
related plants	The forms usually grown are 'Albescens', with vertical green and cream stripes, and 'Zebrina', horizontally striped with white

TUFTED SEDGE
(Carex elata 'Aurea', syn. *C. stricta* 'Bowles' *Golden')*

Many sedges are too tall and robust for all but the largest ponds, or plain green and uninspiring. This is one of the small handful of shorter and non-invasive variegated sedges that provide good year-round interest.

type	Hardy evergreen perennial sedge; bog and marginal plant
height	45cm (18in)
spread	60cm (2ft)
position	Full sun, tolerates light shade, in any moist soil, and in water, depth 0–5cm (0–2in), in a bog garden (including temporarily dry areas) and at the margins of larger ponds
care	Plant autumn or spring, 30cm (12in) apart, in neat groups. Feed in spring with a general fertilizer. Leave the topgrowth over winter and cut down towards mid-spring
propagation	Division in autumn or spring, every 5–6 years
related plants	*C. riparia* 'Variegata', of similar size, has green/white striped leaves; *C. hachijoensis* 'Evergold' has broader flattened leaves with creamy yellow variegation

REEDMACE, BULRUSH
(Typha laxmannii)

Neither true reeds nor rushes, but recognised by everyone as the familiar 'bulrushes'. Whereas the normal kinds are enormous and wildly invasive, this one is typical of the more restrained species suitable for garden ponds.

type	Hardy evergreen perennial; bog and marginal plant, and shallow water aquatic
height	75–90cm (30–36in)
spread	90cm (36in)
position	Full sun or very light shade, in moist or wet soil, and water, depth 0–15cm (0–6in)
care	Plant in spring, 60cm (2ft) apart in groups beside large ponds, or singly in baskets in smaller ones. Deadhead after flowering if seedlings are not wanted, and cut down foliage in late autumn
propagation	Division every 3–4 years in spring
related plants	*T. minima*, only 50 × 20cm (20 × 8in), is a miniature reedmace, ideal for small ponds

PURPLE MOOR GRASS
(Molinia caerulea 'Variegata'*)*

All molinias are tough and adaptable grasses, even withstanding drought, and noted for their supple foliage that turns bright gold in autumn. This variety is best for gardens, with its compact size, neat habit, and attractive white-edged leaves and plumes of violet-blue flowers

type	Hardy semi-evergreen perennial grass; bog and marginal plant
height	75cm (30in)
spread	50cm (20in)
position	Full sun or light shade, in acid soil on sites ranging from slightly damp bog gardens to pond margins, in water, depth 0–10cm (0–4in)
care	Plant in spring, 30cm (12in) apart, in bold drifts. Feed with a general fertilizer in spring. Clumps need dividing only after many years
propagation	Division in spring
related plants	'Moorhexe' has fine black flower plumes; *Sesleria autumnalis* and *S. heufleriana* (Green Moor Grass) are good alternatives for alkaline soils, with silvery white and black plumes respectively

(back) 'Zebrina' form of striped club rush; (front l to r) tufted sedge; purple moor grass and bulrush

practical project

MAKING WATER FLOW: 3

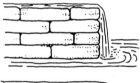

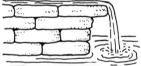

A soft trickle of water (top) becomes a torrent if you create an overhang

WATERFALLS

A waterfall is a dramatic feature that combines the charm and vitality of a flowing stream with the sound and light of a fountain. Depending on the design and construction, water can be made to spill gently over a shallow sill, thunder like a vigorous cataract from a high ledge or sparkle and ripple brightly down a cascade of shallow rocky rapids.

Unfortunately, it is very easy to be over-ambitious at the planning stage. A torrent crashing into a pool far below might be exciting at first but can become noisily intrusive if the sound of softly trickling water is all that is required. It would also need a lot of time and expense to build, and in most gardens could be hopelessly out of scale, for a waterfall makes a very strong statement, dominating its setting and easily overwhelming other features. Your design should always take into account the lie of the land – a high mound or tall rock outcrop built in the middle of level ground will always look artificial – as well as the character of the rest of the garden. Choose materials that are sympathetic to nearby buildings or paved surfaces, and remember that turbulent water is disliked by many pond fish and plants (see margin).

A TERRACOTTA WATERFALL

In a small garden or paved area, an enchanting water feature can be made by using a large, or even broken, clay pot or urn as the header pool and allowing the circulating

CALCULATING THE FLOW

As with fountains (see p122), some preliminary calculations are necessary to ensure success when designing a waterfall.

■ *Match the head of water (the height from which it falls) to the size of pump: the higher the waterfall, the lower the output from a particular pump model. This is also reduced by a long or devious run of delivery pipe and by using a pipe with a narrow bore.*

■ *The ideal rate of pumping is about 1–1½ times the volume of the pond or catchment tank every hour. As an example, a pond with a capacity of 1800 litres (400 gallons) will need a pump rating of 1800–2400 litres (400–600 gallons) per hour.*

■ *To create an authentic sheet of water flowing over the fall requires about 270 litres (60 gallons) per hour for every 2.5cm (1in) width of the sill. So a 10cm (4in) wide waterfall will need a flow of about 1080 litres (240 gallons) per hour.*

■ *For maximum effect, keep dimensions small. For the average garden, a head or vertical distance of 90cm (3ft) from the bottom to the top of the fall is adequate. Limit the width of sills over which the water flows to about 15cm (6in), and step each level of a cascade down 30cm (12in) at the most – even a drop of 10cm (4in) can make an attractive waterfall.*

water to fall into a pebbled area concealing a catchment tank that also houses the pump.

Sink a water tank or dig out a pit for lining with plastic sheeting as described for a pebble fountain on p124, and cover with wire mesh that is strong enough to support a bed of pebbles. Arranging this bed in a shallow depression lined with plastic sheeting will extend the catchment area and reduce potential water loss from splashing.

To one side of this bed set the pot at an angle, if necessary bedding it in mortar for stability. Feed the delivery pipe from the pump through the drainage hole and make the fitting watertight with a rubber grommet (available from water garden suppliers). Plant a few ferns nearby to complete the cool peaceful effect.

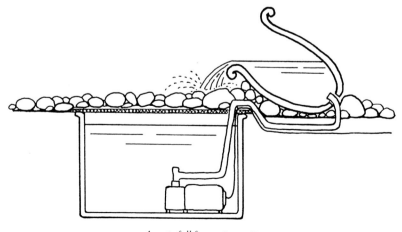

A waterfall from a terracotta urn

BUILDING A WATERFALL

The same three main construction materials are available for waterfalls as for streams: concrete, flexible liners (p119) and preformed units.

Concrete is heavy to lay, but offers an ideal medium for bedding rocks and gravel and for making sills or ledges. Give the finished surface 2–3 coats of sealing paint and flush thoroughly with water to remove any toxic chemicals before use.

A flexible liner is easy to install and adapt to your own design, and is perhaps the best option for informal layouts. The material is laid in the same way as for a stream (see p118–19), but in sections, using a separate piece for each catchment basin. Start work at the bottom and work upwards, overlapping each successive piece over the one below by at least 30cm (12in); the joints may be sealed

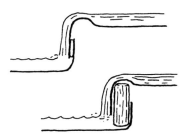

Methods of joining flexible liners using mastic (top) and by wrapping the ends round treated timber (below)

with mastic to prevent capillary seepage, or you can wrap the ends of the liner around rocks or treated timber such as sections of railway sleepers set to form a ledge or weir.

INSTALLING A RIGID WATERFALL UNIT

Preformed units in fibreglass and reconstituted stone are available, as a complete header/catchment pool system with a single intervening ledge, and also as linked modules that can be arranged in various ways to create cascades with or without linking stream sections. They are all laid in the same way.

■ Mark the overall outline on the ground, together with the position of joints between units where appropriate.

■ Dig out the holes, allowing an extra 10cm (4in) all round each unit; check the levels, especially from side to side.

■ Line the holes with about 8cm (3in) layer of sand.

■ Test each unit in position, starting from the bottom, and add or remove sand until they nestle tightly together with full overlaps.

■ Install the pump in the catchment pond and lay the delivery pipe to the header pool.

■ Fill the catchment pond with water and turn on the pump at full force to check the flow and path of the water.

■ Adjust its path by adding pebbles or rocks: experiment with their positioning in the centre and at the edges of the bed and also around the sills.

■ When you are satisfied, backfill around the units with soil, sand or concrete as appropriate, and settle this in thoroughly.

■ Finally, conceal the edges of the units and the delivery pipe with stones, turf or plants, and mortar in place any stones that might be disturbed by the flowing water.

PLANTS IN WATER COURSES
Many aquatic plants dislike moving water, so you should choose carefully when planting near streams, fountains and waterfalls. Spray from fountains is particularly injurious to water lilies and other large-leaved deep water aquatics, which are unable to photosynthesize and so rot quickly if their upper surfaces are constantly wet; they also prefer still water and resent turbulence at the roots. A fountain with a bell or tulip jet creates the least disturbance, and a small gently flowing waterfall may be acceptable if the water lands first on a bed of pebbles or gravel from which it can seep into the lily pond. Most marginals and submerged plants accept some water movement, cautious experiment revealing exactly how much they will tolerate.

Layout of rigid units to create a waterfall

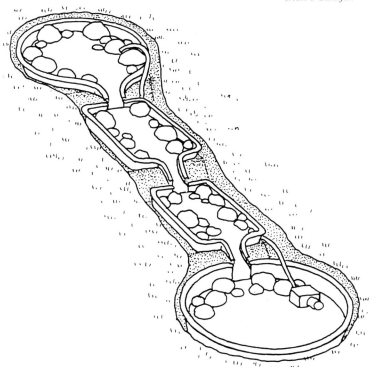

USEFUL ADDRESSES

SOCIETIES

British Dragonfly Society
1 Haydn Avenue
Purley
Surrey CR8 4AG

Issues instructive booklets on creating and managing pond habitats for dragonflies

British Trust for Conservation Volunteers
36 St Mary's St
Wallingford
Oxon OX10 0EU

Various leaflets and practical activities as part of their national Pond Campaign

Field Studies Council
Preston Montford
Montford Bridge
Shrewsbury
Salop SY4 1HW

Organizes many courses, often for families, exploring various aspects of ponds and pond life

International Water Lily Society

(for address, see Stapeley Water Gardens under Suppliers) Furthers interest in all aspects of water gardening, not just water lilies

Japanese Garden Society
Tatton Park
Knutsford
Cheshire WA16 6QN

Advice on creating and conserving oriental gardens

The Wildlife Trusts
The Green, Witham Park
Waterside South
Lincoln LN5 7JR

Umbrella organization co-ordinating the work of county Wildlife Trusts, most of which are involved in pond campaigns and can also arrange environmental surveys

If any water habitat, whether a pond or flowing water course, appears to be polluted, report the details to the Environmental Agency, (01454) 624414

SUPPLIERS

Beaver Water Plant & Fish Farm
Eastbourne Rd
Newchapel
Lingfield
Surrey RH7 6HL

Lotus Water Garden Products
Junction St
Burnley
Lancs BB12 0NA

Stapeley Water Gardens
London Rd
Stapeley
Nantwich
Cheshire CW5 7LH

Wildwoods Water Gardens
Theobalds Park Rd
Crews Hill
Enfield
Middx EN2 9BP

Wychwood Carp Farm
Farnham Rd
Odiham
Nr Basingstoke
Hants RG25 1HS

FURTHER READING

Aquatic Plants in Britain and Ireland Preston/Croft (Harley Books, Colchester, 1997). Botanical account, family by family, of all the native species, produced for the Environmental Agency.

Backyard Fish Farming Bryant, Jauncey & Atack (Prism Press, 1990). Although written for self-sufficient gardeners, one of the best guides to raising fish in ponds.

The Complete Book of the Water Garden Swindells/Mason (Ward Lock, 1989). Limited illustrations of plants, but filled with creative ideas and practical hints.

The Damp Garden Beth Chatto (Dent, 1986). A remarkable practical guide to over 1000 plants for different kinds of damp habitats.

The Stream Garden Arscott/Skinner (Ward Lock, 1994). Creative ideas for flowing water in natural settings.

The Water Garden Frances Perry (Van Nostrand, 1981). An inspired classic that has never been excelled.

INDEX

Numbers in *italic* refer to illustrations

Acorus calamus, 130, *130*
Aeration, 132
Ajuga reptans, 34
Alder, 13, *13*
Algae, 53
Alisma plantago-aquatica,
96, *97*
Alnus glutinosa 'Imperialis',
13, *13*
American bog arum, 43, *43*
Amphibious bistort, 31, *31*
Aponogeton distachyos, 91,
116
Aquatic plants
deep-water, 48, 114;
buying, 53, dividing,
41
floating, 48, 114, 120,
120–1; dividing, 41;
thinning, 76
for indoor ponds, 133
planting, 52, *52*
Arrow arum, 66
Arrowhead, 78, *78*
Arum lily, 114,116, *116*
Aruncus dioicus, 116, *116*
Aspen, weeping, 13, *13*
Astilbe, 79, *79*
Astilbe x *arendsii,* 79, *79*
Azolla filiculoides, syn.
A. caroliniana, 120, *121*

Bamboos, 83, *83*
Baskets, planting in, 40, 49,
52, *52*
Beach, pebble, 58, *58*
Bedding plants, 137
Betula pendula 'Youngii',
13, *13*
Birch, weeping, 13, *13*
Birds, 98
Bladderwort, 120, *120*;
propagation of winter
buds, 103, *103*
Blanketweed, 64, 65, *65*
Bog arum, 54, *54*
Bog asphodel, 97, *97*
Bog bean, *54*, 55; division,
29
Bog gardens, 68–9
hydroponic, 68–9, *69*
irrigated, 68, *68*
mulching, 136
overflow, 68, *68*
planting, 41, 114
weeding, 76–7
Bog plants, 41, 48, 114;
dividing, 41
Brass buttons, 31, *31*
Bridges, 106–7;
maintenance, 137
Brooklime, 66, *66*
Bugle (common), 34
Bulrush, 138, *139*
Butomus umbellatus, 78,
78

Caddisfly, *99;* larvae, 102

Calla lily, 116, *116*
Calla palustris, 54, *54*
Callitriche hermaphroditica,
syn. *C. autumnalis,* 23,
23
Caltha palustris, 42
Camassia leichtlinii, 61, *61*
Canadian pondweed, 22
Cardamine pratensis, 46
Cardinal flower, 104, *104*
Carex elata 'Aurea', syn.
C. stricta 'Bowles'
Golden', 138, *139*
Ceratophyllum demersum,
22
Chinese garden, 80
Chinese loosestrife, 84, *84*
Clay, puddled, 16, 28, 56,
69, *69*
Composts, 49
Concrete
mixing, 32
quantities of, calculating,
33
stream course, 118–19,
119
when to lay, 115
Corkscrew rush, 138, *138*
Cotton grass, 67, *67*
Cotula coronopifolia, 31, *31*
Cuckoo flower, 46, *46*
Curled pondweed, 22, *22*
Cuttings, 111, *111*
Cyperus longus, 15

Darmera peltata, syn.
Peltiphyllum peltatum,
30, *30*
Day lily, 66, *66*
Decking, wooden, 106,
maintenance, 137
Deep-water aquatics, 48,
114; buying, 53; dividing,
41
Deer scarer, 82, *82*
Division, 110 *see also
individual species*
Dragonflies, 98, *98*
Duckweed, 10, 65, *65*, 120
Duck potato, 78, *78*

East Indian lotus, 131, *131*;
overwintering, 114–15,
114
Edgings, 32–3, *33*, 45, *45*,
58–9, *59*; plants for, 59
Eichornia crassipes, syn.
Pontederia crassipes ,
14, 114
Electricity, 86, *86*
Eleocharis acicularis, 22
Elodea canadensis, 22
Equipment, maintenance,
40, 128
Equisetum hyemale, syn.
E. hibernale, 14, *14*
Eriophorum angustifolium,
67, *67*

Eupatorium cannabinum,
108, *108*

Fairy moss, 120, *121*
Ferns, 119
Filipendula ulmaria, 60, *60*
Filters, 87
Filtration, 132
Fish, 12, 13, 72–3, *73*, 90
casualties, 90–1
feeding, 41, 103
fry, 90, *90*
koi carp, 72, *73*, 83
Floating aquatics, 48, 114,
120, *120–1*; dividing 29;
thinning, 76
Flowering rush, 78, *78*
Fontinalis antipyretica, 23,
23
Fountains, 118, 122–5,
122–3, 125
Fringed water lily, 104, *105*
Fritillaria meleagris, 46
Frogbit, 120, *121*;
propagation of winter
buds, 103, *103*
Frogs, 65, 98, *99*, 128;
disease in, 103; lifecycle,
41

Gentiana pneumonanthe,
34, *34*
Geum rivale, 61, *61*
Globe flower, 54, *54*
Glyceria maxima, syn.
*G. aquatica, G.
spectabilis,* 30, *30*
Goat's beard, 116, *116*
Golden buttons, 31, *31*
Golden club, 42, *42*
Golden rays, 109, *109*
Goldfish weed, 22, *22*
Grasses, rushes and
sedges, 138–9, *139*, 115
Greater spearwort, 85, *85*
'Green' water, 53, 64
Gunnera manicata, 114,
117, *117*

Hairgrass, 22
Hardy pond lilies, 70
Hardy water lilies, 70, 71,
71
Heaters, 87
Heating, costs, 132
Heloniopsis, 34, *35*
Heloniopsis orientalis, syn.
H. japonica, 34
Hemerocallis cultivars, 66,
66
Hemp agrimony, 108, *108*
Herons, 53
Himalayan cowslip, 92
Hoop petticoat, 47, *47*
Hornwort, 22
Horse-tail, 22, *22*
Hosta fortunei, 105,*105*
Hottonia palustris, 23

Houseplants, for indoor
ponds, 133
Houttuynia, 60
Houttuynia cordata, 60, *60*
Hydrocharis morsus-ranae,
120, *121*
Hypericum elodioides, syn.
H. elodes, 109

Indoor pond *see* Ponds,
indoor
Iris laevigata, 104, *104*
Iris sibirica, 96, *96*
Islands, 59, *59;* plants for,
59

Japanese garden, 80, *80–1*
Japanese water iris, 104,
104
Juncus effusus 'Spiralis',
138, *138*

Kaffir lily, 131, *131*
Kingcup, 42, *42*

Lagarosiphon major,
syn. *Elodea crispa,* 22
Lavender musk, 108, *108*
Leaves,
as shelter for wildlife, 98
dealing with, 13, 40, 102,
102
Leafmould, 128
Leaf stacks, 128
Leeches, 76, *76*
Lemna trisulca, 120
Leucojum vernum, 35, *35*
Ligularia, 109, *109*
Ligularia dentata, 109, *109*
Lighting, 87, 107
Liners, 16
flexible, 16, 37, 56, 119,
132
repairing, 37, *37*
rigid, 16, 37, 132;
installing, 44–5, *45;*
maintaining, 45
Lizard's tail, 84, *84*
Lobelia cardinalis, 104, *104*
Lungwort, 47, *47*
Lychnis flos-cuculi, 85, *85*
Lysichiton americanus, syn.
Lysichitum americanum,
43, *43*
Lysimachia clethroides, 84,
84
Lythrum salicaria, 84, *84*

Marginals, 29, 48; buying,
53; dividing, 29
Marsh gentian, 34
Marsh marigold, 42, *42*
Marsh St John's wort, 109
Marsh trefoil, 54, *55;*
division, 29
Mayflies, 53
Meadowsweet, 60
Mentha aquatica, 96, *97*

INDEX

Menyanthes trifoliata, 55
Mimulus ringens, 108, *108*
Miriophyllum spicatum, 23, *23*
Molinia caerulea 'Variegata', 139, *139*
Mulching, 114, 128, 137
Mussels, freshwater, *99*
Myosotis scorpioides, syn. *M. palustris,* 43, *43*

Narcissus bulbocodium, 47, *47*
Narthecium ossifragum, 97, *97*
Nelumbo nucifera, 131, *131*; overwintering, 114–15, *115*
Newts, 98, *99*
Nuphar spp., 70, *70*
Nymphaea spp., 70
Nymphoides peltata, 104, *105*

Ornamental rhubarb, 55, *55*
Orontium aquaticum, 42
Osier, weeping purple, 13, *13*
Osmunda regalis, 130, *130*
Overflows, 107, *107*
Oxygenators, 22–3, *22–3,* 114; buying, 53

Peltandra undulata, syn. *P. virginica,* 66
Perennials, dividing, 41; planting, 114
Persicaria amphibia, syn. *Polygonum amphibium,* 31, *31*
Pests, 53, 64, 98
Pickerel weed, *78,* 79
Pistia stratiotes, 15
Planning, 136, *see also Ponds, planning*
Plantain lily, 105, *105*
Planting, 110–11, *110, 111*
Planting plans, 49; 136
Plants
    bamboos, 83, *83*
    bedding, 137
    bog 41, 48, 114; choosing new, 15, 49, 52–3; dividing, 41; planting, 114
    checking for pests, 53
    deep-water aquatics, 48, 114; buying, 45; dividing, 41
    feeding, 40, *40*
    ferns for streams, 119
    floating aquatics, 114, 120, *120–1;* dividing, 41; thinning, 76
    for edging, 59
    for formal ponds, 32
    for indoor ponds, 133
    for islands, 59
    for miniature ponds
    for rock gardens, 28
    in water courses, 141
    marginals, 29, 114;

buying, 45; dividing, 41
oriental gardens, 82
oxygenators, 22–3, *22–3,* 114; buying, 53
protection, 12, *12*
raised for patios, 95, *95*
watering, 110
Pond lilies, hardy, 70
Pond skaters, *99*
Ponds *see also* Aeration, Filtration and Heating
    cleaning, 13, 36, 40
    concrete, 12, 16, 32–3; *33;* repairing, 37, *37*
    costs of, 17
    dimensions, 16
    edgings, 32–3, *33*
    emptying, 103
    excavation, 24–5, *25,* 28
    filling, 48
    formal, 17, *17;* constructing, 32–3; plants for, 32
    frozen, 12
    indoor, 132–3, *133*
    informal, 17, *17;* creating, 44–5; planting, 45, 48–9, *49*
    liners *see* Liners
    marking out, 24, *24*
    miniature, 94–5, *94*
    oriental, 80–3, *80–1*
    planning new, 16–17, 32, 44, 56, 80
    plants for, *see* Plants *and individual species*
    repairing, 12, 36–7
    restoring, 36–7, *37*
    shape, 16–17
    topping up, 28–9, 40
    wildlife, 56–9, *57, 98, 98*
Pontederia cordata, 78, 79
Populus tremulus, 'Pendula', 13, *13*
Potamogeton crispus, 22, *22*
Prickly rhubarb (giant), 114, 117, *117*
Primula, 92–3, *92–3;*
    drumstick, 92
    orchid, 93
    P. aurantiaca, 92
    P. beesiana, 92
    P. x *bulleesiana,* 92
    P. denticulata, 92, *93*
    P. florindae, 92
    P. japonica, 6–7, 8–9, 92, *92*
    P. pulverulenta, 93, *93*
    P. rosea, 93, *93*
    P. sikkimensis, 93, *93*
    P. vialii, 93, *93*
    sowing, 41
Propagation, 110–11; of shrubs, 128–9, *129; see also individual species*
Protection, plant, 12, *12,* 114
    of small ponds, 128
Pulmonaria angustifolia, 47, *47*
Pumps, 87, *87,* 119, 122, 124, *124*

Purple loosestrife, 84, *84*
Purple moor grass, 139, *139*

Quamash, 61, *61*

Ragged robin, 85, *85*
Ranunculus aquatilis, 23, *23*
Ranunculus lingua 'Grandiflorus', 85, *85*
Reedmace, 138, *139*
Rheum palmatum, 55, *55*
River lily, 131, *131*
Rock gardens, 28, *28*
    plants for, 28
    protection from falling leaves, 102
Rodgersia, 67, *67*
Rodgersia tabularis, syn. *Astilboides tabularis,* 67, *67*
Royal fern, 130, *130*

Safety, 7, 87, 91
Sagittaria sagittifolia, syn. *S. japonica,* 78, *78*
Salix caprea 'Kilmarnock', 13, *13; S. daphnoides* 'Aglaia', 13, *13, S. purpurea* 'Pendula', 13, *13*
Saururus cernuus, 84, *84*
Schoenoplectus lacustris subsp. *tabernaemontani,* 138, *139*
Schyzostylis coccinea, 131, *131*
Scouring rush (Dutch), 14, *14*
Seasons, 9
Shelves, marginal, 111
Shrimps, freshwater, *99*
Shrubs, 115
    planting, 137, *137*
    propagating, 128–9, *129*
Siberian iris, 96, *96*
Skunk cabbage, 43, *43*
Snails, 65, *65,* 98, *99*
    eggs, 53
    ram's-horn, 53, *99*
Snakeshead fritillary, 46
Sowing seeds, 111, *111*
Spiked milfoil, 23, *23*
Spring snowflake, 35, *35*
Stepping stones, 107; maintenance, 137
Stratiotes aloides, 121, *121*
Streams, 118–19, *119*
Striped club rush, 138, *139*
Sweet flag, 130, *130*
Sweet galingale, 15

Toad-spawn, 29, *29*
Trapa natans, 121, *121*
Trees, 16, 36, 115
    ornamental, 13, *13*
    planting, 137, *137*
Trollius europaeus, 54, *54*
Tufted sedge, 138, *139*
Turions (winter buds), 103, *103*
Typha laxmannii, 138, *139*

Umbrella plant, 30
Underwater viewer, 91, *91*
Utricularia vulgaris, 120, *120*

Veronica beccabunga, 66, *66*

Water
    acid/alkaline test, *40*
    calculating flow, 119, 140
    carbon dioxide in, 91
    'green', 53, 64
    levels, 12, 107; topping up, 28–9
    jet, 122, 124
    nitrate levels, 41
    oxygen in, 76, 90–1
    polluted, 36
    quality, 40, 41
Water avens, 61, *61*
Water beetles, 65
Water buttercup, 23, *23*
Water chestnut, 121, *121*
Water crowfoot, 23, *23*
Water forget-me-not, 43, *43*
Water fringe, 104, *105*
Water grass, 30, *30*
Water hawthorn, 91, 116
Water hyacinth, 14, 114
Water lettuce, 15
Water lilies, 70–1
    care, 90
    dividing, 4, 53, *53*
    fringed, 104
    hardy, 70, 71, *71*
    overwintering, 115
    propagation, 77, *77,* 111, *111*
    top dressing, 29, *29*
    tropical, 70
    velocity, 119, *119*
Water mint, 96, *97;* division, 96
Water plantain, 96, *97*
Water soldier, 121, *121*
Water spiders, 65, *99*
Water starwort, 23, *23*
Water violet, 23; planting, 23
Waterfalls, 118, 140–1, *141*
Watering, 77, 110
Weeding, 68, 76–7
Weedkillers, 136
Whirligig beetle, 77, *77*
Wildflower meadow, 69, *69*
Wildflowers, 9
Wildlife, 9, 10, 36, *41,* 53, 76, 77, 98–9, *98, 99,* 102, 128
    insects, 64, 65, *65*
    plants to attract, 99
    pond, 56–9, *57*
Willow, 13, *13;* violet, 13, *13*
Willow moss, 23, *23*

Zantedeschia aethiopica, 114, 116